We All

Chase

Rainbows.

By Ivin Munson.

Marie;
The name on the cover is misspelled but that doesn't change the text. Someday, when you can slow down like I have, you can sit in your rocking chair & read this. Hope to see you at our 50th class reunion, Love ya. Enjoy & God Bless.
Ivin

Dedicated to my dear wife Irene, who kept me going when
I was ready to quit.

We All Chase Rainbows

Published as a Watchmaker Publishing paperback 2001,
Watchmaker Publishing, Ltd.

ISBN 0-9709917-8-9

Printed and bound in the United States of America

1 2 3 4 5 6 7 8 9 0

Prologue

"I reckon that like most stories I've been told, this one ought ta start with, 'Once upon a time.' The difference is, this ain't no ordinary story 'cause this one's true. I know 'cause it's about me 'n my kin. My name's Timothy B. Baxter, 'n I'm twelve years old. Well nearly twelve anyhow. My birthday's in just five more months 'n that puts me closer ta twelve than it does ta eleven. Pa always tells me ta not wish my life away, but he don't remember what it's like ta be my age. Then a feller's too old ta get away with shenanigans, 'n too young ta gets ta stay up late. Sometimes I wonder if Pa was ever a kid. He tells of the things he did when he was young, 'n boy am I sick of hearin' 'bout the old days. I know he's getting' old, why he must be pushin' forty or even forty-five by now, but after all this is eighteen hundred 'n fifty-nine. The old days are gone forever 'n these here are modern times. Why I bet there ain't nothin' that anybody can come up with that's new.

Like I said, 'My name's Timothy B. Baxter,' but most folks call me just plain, 'Tim'. Everybody that is, 'ceptin' Ma 'n, she insists on callin' me, 'Timothy'. I don't tell nobody what the, 'B,' stands fer but ol' Ma let it out 'a the bag one day. Seems she was upset with me fer somethin' or the other, 'n I'll be blamed if she didn't stand on the porch 'n holler at the top a her lungs. 'Timothy Bacon Baxter you get home this very minute.' Well, as soon as she done that my goose was cooked. Now every kid in town knew my middle name was, 'Bacon,' 'n did I catch it from then on. Why I was called everythin' from, 'Ham hocks" to "Pork belly,' to 'Hog jowls.' Bacon was Ma's maiden name 'n they give me that as a middle name. Don't know why Pa couldn't have married somebody named somethin' simple like 'Thomas,' or 'Smith,' or somethin' like that. I love my Ma, I really do, but I could love her just as much without a name that gets me called, 'Ol' Pork Chops,' all the time. Had ta do a lot a fightin' after Ma blabbed ta the whole neighborhood what my middle name was. I sure ain't gonna hang a moniker like that on no kid a mine.

Pa's a blacksmith, here in town 'n a dad-blamed good one. Only problem is he's got the wanderlust 'n everything's gonna be better just over the next hill. Him 'n Ma started out in Illinois, moved ta upper Ohio, then on ta Kentuck' 'n Mississip'. When my older brother came along Ma told Pa ta make up his mind where he was gonna settle, 'cause she couldn't be packin' a bunch a kids all over the continent. There'd been rumblin's of war, for lots 'a years, 'tween the slave states 'n the abolitionists up north. Pa didn't have no feelin's one way or t'other. All he wanted was ta be left alone ta raise his family, which grew ta three with the twins comin' along. Some fella told him 'bout free land out west 'n that's how we ended up here in Hannibal, Missouri. Pa got forty acres of land that he has a hard time even growin' rocks on, let alone crops, so he opened up his Smithy shop in town 'n tries ta farm too. I got born on the trip west, on June eleventh, eighteen hundred and forty seven. I reckon Ma took one look at me 'n decided ta call it quits, 'cause there weren't no more kids after me.

Pa straddled the fence on the slave issue as long as he could, but lately his blacksmith business has been fallin' off. Missouri had come inta the Union as a slave state but there's a whole bunch a abolitionists here too. They quit doin' business with Pa 'cause he wouldn't take a stand against slavery, 'n them that's for slavery quit comin' in 'cause they thought he was again' it. Seems like Pa can't win no matter what. I reckon that about brings ya up ta date on the past. What ever happens from now on, only the Good Lord Knows."

by Timothy B. Baxter.

CHAPTER ONE.

"Things ain't gettin' much better in Congress 'n there's gonna be a shootin' war sure as I'm sittin' here. More territories are openin' up out west, 'n there's even talk of the states that favor slavery breakin' away from the Union 'n formin' a new nation," said Chad Baxter as he casually tossed the fishing line into the river. He, his twin brother Tad and younger brother Tim were supposed to be in school, however the day was way too nice to listen to Old Lady Hemmingway spout off, so they cut for the fishing hole. "Pa 'n Ma can see good 'n bad in both sides but kind'a favor the South," Tim added to the conversation, shifting the cane pole to his other hand and slapped at a mosquito that had landed on his bare arm. "As for me, what does a twelve year old know 'bout politics? Never owned a slave 'n don't intend ta, but at the same time Pa says that some factories up north ain't much more than slave shops themselves. Reckon it depends whose eyes yer lookin' at it through. Either way it don't bother me much. Long as the catfish are bitin' 'n I can still go frog giggin' I'm happy. Would like the summers ta be a bit longer 'n school a lot shorter though."

"A lot shorter is right," laughed Tad. "Can't see what good knowin' the A B C's is gonna do when some Yankee soldier's shootin' minnie balls at yer head. When it does break out, what side do ya think Ma 'n Pa's gonna take? Ma's dead again' on any kind a fightin', 'n Pa figures that what they do back east ain't none a his business long as they leave him alone."

The twins were two years older than Tim, and he was always the butt of their jokes and often down right mean tricks. "But," they argued, "what good is havin' a younger brother if ya can't pick on him?" Somehow that type of thinking never made much sense to the one on the receiving end.

While the twins bantered back and fourth, about what they were going to do when the impending war came, Tim silently watched the bobber as it made concentric rings in the water. There hadn't been so much as a nibble for over an hour and the sun was getting close to where they had to head for home. If they were late their parents would know they hadn't spent the day in school 'n boy would there be trouble then. Hiding the long cane poles in the willows, just in case tomorrow will be as nice as today was, the three trotted for home. Cutting through pastures and over fences they made certain that they were approaching the house from the direction of the school. Once they made the mistake of coming from the river side and Mrs. Baxter had seen them. There was no use lying to Ma when she flat out asked them if they had been fishing. The worst part of the punishment was the period of time they had to wait for their father to get home. The licking didn't cure them of cutting school; it merely served to make them more cautious in the future.

By the time they turned down the road leading to their cabin, both Tad and Chad had decided they would join the Confederate army. Arm in arm the twins sashayed down the path, leaving their younger brother behind. "Why, with us two fightin' them Yankees the war'll be over in a couple weeks," Chad boasted. "Reckon if we put our minds to it we could kill five or six apiece before breakfast."

"Why stop at five or six? Make it an even dozen 'n work up a real man's appetite," Tad replied, not wanting to be outdone by his twin. "Only sad thing 'bout us leavin' for war is that Chet'll go too. That leaves only Tim ta help Pa around the farm, 'n we all know how much help he is. 'bout like havin' a ol' blind, three legged mule a pullin' the plow. Feel sorry for Pa, but I reckon even Tim's better 'en nothin', or nothin's better 'en Tim, don't know which."

"You two join up with the Confederates 'n I know fer a fact that they'll lose fer sure. "If y'all don't shut yer big mouths, I'm gonna have Chet kick the stuffin' out 'a both 'a y'all." Tim tried to sound as menacing as possible.

Chet was a year and a half-older than the twins and protected Tim from the other two, when he wasn't picking on the younger one himself that is. A bit over sixteen years old he naturally had himself a girlfriend. When Tim asked him to cut school and go fishing with them his answer was, "What, 'n miss a chance ta sit next ta Cynthia? You must be daft ta think I'd chase some dumb ol' catfish 'stead a that."

While Cynthia Harris was pretty enough, and every boy in town was chasing after her, to Tim there was something definitely wrong with his brother's priorities. After all, there would always be girls around, but good fishing days are few and far between. Deep down he hoped that he would never have to give up his fishing just for some female. What could a girl have to offer that a fella couldn't find in relaxing by the riverbank? Tim was so absorbed in this dilemma that he hadn't noticed that the twins had stopped in the doorway and ran into them, knocking them into the room. Both parents were sitting at the table, a steaming cup of chicory before them. It was unusual for Pa to be home this early, even though business at the blacksmith shop was almost nonexistent.

"I didn't realize it was that late," Ma said, breaking her conversation with Pa off in mid sentence. Her hands seemed to shake as she brought the cup to her lips. Setting the cup down she studied her boys with a look that none of them could remember seeing before. Was it possible she knew something that they didn't particularly want her to know? "How was school today, boys?"

The question riveted all three in their tracks. "Okay," they answered in unison, afraid to look in her direction. Ma had an uncanny way of looking right through a person and into their very soul. Her piercing eyes had caught them in fibs more than once, and with Pa here they didn't want it to happen now. They breathed a collective sigh of relief as Chet ran into the room, nearly tearing the wooden door from its hasp.

"Is that the way you were taught to enter a room?" Pa's voice had a harder edge than customary. "You liked ta scared your Ma half ta death. Now go out 'n come in like you're supposed ta 'n be quick about it. Dad-blamed kids think this place's a saloon they can bust up anytime they want."

Gasping to catch his breath, Chet merely stood in the doorway. "Pa..." he uttered between gasps. "They went 'n done it. Those blamed fools went 'n elected that new slave lovin' Republican Party

ta office." Chet advanced to the table and laid today's copy of the
Hannibal newspaper. "With that skinny stovepipe Lincoln in the
White House we're goin' ta war sure. He promised ta outlaw slavery 'n there's a bunch 'a Southern states gonna be mighty sore
'bout this. Says here in the paper that some might even break from
the Union 'n be a separate country. Jeb Tollifson, down at the paper, says South Carolina is makin' plans ta do just that 'n right soon
too. We got no notion 'bout what's happened now. 'less it comes
over the clicker at the telegraph office, it's more 'n a weeks time
'fore we get the news here."

Holding up his hand for silence Lorenzo Baxter put on his spectacles, picked up the paper from the table and walked to the window where the light was better. Everyone waited with baited breath
until he closed the paper and returned to his chair. "I'd heard ru-
mors 'bout this in town. That's one reason I'm home early. Your
Ma 'n I were discussing what we're gonna do 'n it's our plan ta do
nothin'. We are just plain folks that just want ta be left alone. Never
held much with slavery, but don't like the government tellin' others
what they can 'n can't do with their property. If they're allowed ta
get away with it now there ain't gonna be no end ta what laws
they'll pass. Just nip a bit here 'n a bit there 'n soon they'll control
'bout everythin' a body does, 'cept breathin'. If there's a shootin'
war we'll ride the fence, same as we always have. But I ain't
gonna have no son 'a mine killed over some black slave a million
miles away in South Carolina."

"But Pa," Chet protested, "it ain't a million miles away, it's
right next door. Missouri was admitted as a slave state 'n we owe
it ta our brother states ta stand up 'n fight for what's right." His
bravado slipped under the shriveling look from his father.

"Right? You call one man ownin' another man, 'Right?' Sure
Missouri's partly a slave state 'n sure there's slave owners right
here in this county, but there's a lot that's again' slavery too. Are ya
willin' ta shoot your girlfriend's Pa? Ya better be, 'cause I know for
a fact that he's an abolitionist. There's more ta think about besides
some black that was sold inta slavery by one of his own kind back
in Africa. If we get into fightin' there's gonna be cryin' 'n wailin'
like this country ain't never heard before. The only way me or mine
are gonna pick up a rifle against anybody, is to defend what's right-

fully ours. That's the end of this conversation, now lets get supper ready.'"

Chet was not about to let the subject end without having his say in the matter. "How 'bouts if the shoe was on the other foot 'n it was the whites that was owned by the blacks. Would ya allow us ta pack a rifle then? Pa yer talkin' like them blacks are real human people. In the Dred Scott Decision, even the Supreme Court says that they're property. The court declared the Missouri Compromise unconstitutional, 'cause it limited what a slave owner could do with his property. Now Pa, ya can't just obey the laws ya like 'n ignore the others. It's the government back east that's breakin' their own laws 'n we have ta stand against 'em. If it comes ta a shootin' war I'm gonna join up with the Confederate States 'n do my part."

There was a deafening silence as Chet finished speaking. Nobody, but nobody, in the family had ever stood up to Pa in this manner. Even Ma skirted around a direct confrontation with her husband. Expecting an explosion like none seen before, everyone was shocked when Pa simply stood up, walked past Chet and went outside. Exchanging puzzled looks everyone was silent for a brief moment. It was Ma who broke the quiet.

"Twins, you set the table while Tim fetches in some wood. Chet, I believe you best go 'n finish your talk with your Pa, 'n a little apologizin' on your part won't hurt none either. He's still your Pa 'n the head 'a this family. You're just barely sixteen 'n you got a lot 'a learnin' ta do. Pa's first thoughts are what's best for us, 'n so far he's raised you boys ta be fine men. He ain't about ta lose one 'a ya over some stupid slave. Before y'all came home he decided that if it came ta war, we'd pack up 'n move west. Ya know Pa 'n his movin' on somewheres else. In the past it's been 'cause there was always somethin' that looked better in the next place. This time it's 'cause he loves all 'a ya too much ta lose ya to some Yankee minnie ball. Pa's seen war 'n, thank the Good Lord, none 'a you have. He's seen men come home without everythin' they left home with. Believe me, Pa's no coward. He just believes any war's senseless 'n just 'cause everyone else's lost their mind, no sign we have ta. Now everybody scat 'n do as I say."

A chastened Chet walked outside, to join his father, while the other boys rushed to do Ma's bidding. Each happy it wasn't them facing Pa right now. They had seen their father in almost every kind of mood, from tears to anger to exuberance. The usually stern face was deceiving, for he was a very kind person at heart. When he was about the age that Tim is now, Pa had been orphaned and raised by his mother's sister. Her husband had packed up and left her, leaving Lorenzo the only male on the place. Her domineering and thankless manner made the lad wonder what had taken his uncle so long to leave? It seemed that no matter how hard a body tried to please her, it was just a bit short of being good enough.

When he finally had all of her abuse and complaining he could take, he too lit out in the dead of night. On his own from the age of thirteen, Lorenzo learned what it was to be hungry, homeless, but most of all, to do what's best for him and his.

Each deep in their individual thoughts the evening meal was unusually quiet. The scrape of forks against the tin plates and an occasional, "Please pass," or "Thank you," was all that broke the silence. It was the rule in this home that no one left the table until Pa lit up his pipe. That was the signal that he was finished eating and one by one the boys excused themselves. Normally Ma and Pa lingered over the final cup of chicory, while the table was cleared and the dishes washed and put away. Tonight there was to be a break in tradition.

"Before anyone leaves the table tonight, there's some things we've gotta clear up." Pa hesitated while he filled the pipe-bowl with shreds of tobacco. "Chet seems ta be set on goin' ta join up when the shootin' starts. I told him how I feel 'bout losin' a son ta war 'n he still wants ta do it." A tear formed in the pale blue eyes and there was a break in his voice as he spoke. "I ain't gonna be one ta dictate what any 'a you should feel inside. The only thing I ask is that ya do a whole lot 'a prayin' 'fore ya jump inta anythin'.

One bullet 'tween the eyes 'n then there's no changin' your minds. So be sure you're makin the right decision. No matter what ya choose to do, or which side ya pick ta back, me 'n Ma 'll stand behind ya. That there door 'll always swing both directions 'n you're always welcome here." With that Pa lit the pipe and the conversation ended.

His father was pouring over the newspaper when Tim sat at

his feet and tugged at the cotton pants leg. "Pa, can I ask ya a question?" Lorenzo laid the paper aside and nodded. "Ma says that ya were thinkin' 'bout movin' west. I heard that there's Indians out there that makes the Arapahos look tame. I really don't want ta go there, so if it's alright with you I'll join up too."

Pa smiled and patted his young son's head. "Don't you worry none 'bout no Indians. We'll do what's best 'n I don't want ta hear no more 'bout my young'un joinin' no army. Why, even the twins are too young ta go fight 'n you're two years younger 'en them. I doubt that they'll even take Chet, seein' as how he's only fifteen."

"Sixteen," Tim corrected his father. "Chet's sixteen last month." Pa scratched his head, while doing some mental figuring.

"Sixteen it is, but that's still way too young for the army ta take him. They want fellas a bit older 'n with experience, men like me."

"Like you?" Tim echoed in mock surprise. "Pa, if they took men your age the whole army would fight in rockin' chairs. It'd be the shortest war in history, 'cause all ya old men'd be too tired ta fight much more 'en an hour or so." Moving quickly Tim barely escaped his father's foot that was aimed at his backside.

"Old man am I? I'll show ya who's an old man, you young whipper-snapper." As fast as he moved, Pa moved faster and soon Tim was the recipient of the dreaded whisker burn to his tender cheeks.

"Uncle," Tim screamed, while the rest of the family laughed at his predicament, "I give Pa, leave me some hide on my face." The rubbing ceased and Tim put his hand to his face, certain that Pa had drawn blood with his rough whiskers.

"You hold him Pa 'n you work one cheek while I work the other," Chet joined the game as a squealing Tim struggled to get away. When Pa relaxed his grip Tim scooted out of his grasp. Dodging Chet's outstretched arms he ran to the opposite side of the table and out of harm's way.

Sticking his tongue out at his brother he added the worst insult that came to mind. "When ya get ta be a man 'n get rid 'a that chicken-fuzz, ya might be able ta give a whisker burn. 'til then it's like havin' a baby's behind rubbed at my face. I bet Cynthia's got more of a beard 'en y'all do." He realized he had pushed a bit too far as Chet rounded the table. Running for the door, Tim barely escaped his brother's grasp as he flew out into the yard, with Chet in close pursuit. The race rounded the well, through the barn and behind the hen house before Tim ran out of breath. The ensuing tickle torture left him yelling for Divine intervention before Chet tired of the game and let Tim up.

"Who's gonna pick on ya when I'm gone ta the war?" Chet asked as he put his arm around his little brother's shoulders. "Lots 'a things I'm gonna miss 'bout this ol' place 'n you're one 'a them. Might have ta take ya with me. Ain't never heard a "Rebel Yell" like the one you done while I was playin' the tune on your ribs back there. No foolin' Tim, I need ya ta take care 'a Ma 'n Pa when I go. Pa thinks the twins are too young, but I got a hunch the Confederates are gonna need everybody ta beat the Blue Bellies. They got three times the men we got 'n a lot more money ta spend on rifles 'n stuff." Arm in arm the bond between the eldest and younger brothers grew as never before. A twinge of apprehension grew in Tim's breast, as he thought of Chet going to where someone may actually shoot at him.

That night, as Tim lay in his bed in the loft, he added an addendum to his regular prayers. "If ya please Lord, make it so there's no war. Things down here don't look too good 'n I don't want nothin' ta happen ta Chet. There ain't all the slaves in this whole country worth losin' my brother over. Ma's told me 'bout that war ya had in Heaven 'n, if it split folks up there as bad as slavery has here, it was terrible. Ma says that the evil ones got throwed out, but there ain't no evil ones down here. It's just that some folks got different ideas than others, 'n there's good 'n bad on both sides. I'd sure appreciate it if ya could see your way clear ta prod them that's thinkin' war 'n change their minds a bit. I reckon that's 'bout all I got ta say for tonight, so Amen." Satisfied that he had done his part to prevent a conflict, Tim closed his eyes and slept soundly.

As each day passed the future looked more and more grim. South Carolina was drawing up Articles of Secession, while others waited on the fringes to see the outcome. With neither side willing to concede to the wishes of the other, the threat of war grew more imminent. The South stood firm in their beliefs that the Union was attempting to coerce them into giving up their property. The Union, on the other hand, would not be satisfied with anything short of total abolishment of slavery. There were many genuine, and just as many half-hearted, attempts in Congress to placate both sides but each failed. Then it happened. Five days before Christmas Day, eighteen hundred and sixty, South Carolina carried out its threat and seceded. Within two months six other states joined South Carolina. Mississippi, Alabama, Texas, Georgia, Florida, Louisiana and South Carolina formed the new Confederate States of America. A graduate of West Point, named Jefferson Davis, was elected president of the newly formed country, which in the near future would add four more states to its flag. The battle lines were drawn and both sides prepared for war. The Confederates began to enlist men for a period of nine months, while the Union for twelve.

Just a few days into the New Year a glowing Chester Baxter entered the house. "I done it, Pa," Chet said, bursting with exuberance. "I signed up, 'n tomorrow I get my uniform when I report ta the courthouse in Hannibal. I can hardly wait for Cynthia ta see me in that spankin' new outfit. I'm gonna be in the Eighth Missouri Regiment." His face flushed with excitement, the lad beamed.

"Is that the reason ya joined the army, ta impress a gal?" Lorenzo dropped the newspaper to the floor and looked deep into his son's eyes. "This here ain't no game, boy. It's gonna be men tryin' to kill each other. This is what I been dreadin' for thirty years, 'cause that's how long it's taken ta come ta this. Them boneheads that make the laws are so durned busy lookin' out for what's best for them, that they let the rest 'a us go ta blazes. This ain't our fight son. It ain't too late ta change your mind 'n we can move out tomorrow. I'll leave everythin' behind 'n we can be gone by sunup."

A look, like none Lorenzo had never seen before, crossed Chet's sunburned face. A combination of rage and frustration turned his face a deeper shade of crimson. "Ya just don't understand, do ya Pa? I ain't one 'a your babies that needs his diaper changed no more. I'm a man now 'n I need ta make my own mind up 'bout things. This might not be your fight, but to me it's more than just about a few slaves. We got ta show the Union that we ain't no longer a stepchild that they can bully. Sure, they're richer 'n bigger 'n got more clout 'en us, but are the factories in the north any more important than our plantations in the south? What if we passed a law that took away their livelihood? Do ya think for a minute they'd stand by 'n let it pass? That's what they're tryin' ta do ta the south. Ya know as well as I do, that if we lose the slaves, there ain't gonna be no more cotton plantations or tobacco farms. If that happens, the mills 'll close 'n there ain't gonna be no more south 'cause we've all starved ta death. If I got a choice 'a starvin' or a bullet, I'll take the bullet. At least then I died fightin' rather than layin' down like ya'll want me to."

There was no reasoning with his son and further arguments were just as futile. "I ain't looked at ya as a baby since ya were a wee lad. I only want ta make sure ya understand how Ma 'n me feel 'bout ya leavin'. You're our firstborn 'n when ya come along there weren't nothin' in this world more important ta us. Back then ya really weren't much ta look at 'n had the personality of a rock.

All ya did was eat, dirty your diapers 'n sleep all day 'n squall all night. If we loved ya that much then, imagine how much we love ya now. You're growed ta a fine young man. One that any man would be proud ta call, 'Son,' 'n I want ta do everythin' in my power ta keep ya by my side. Believe it or not, I do remember when I was your age. I know the chances all young boys take 'n never once think 'bout the consequences. All youngsters believe that nothin' can harm 'em, 'n that bad things always happen ta others. That's why they try ta float across a swolled river ridin' a barrel, or see who can dive off the highest rock inta the swimmin' hole. All kinds 'a things that'd curl your hair just thinkin' 'bout when ya get older. I done it, my Pa done it, you done it, 'n your son 'll do it too.'"

"All my life I ain't never turned a finger against ya 'n I won't start now." Chet was more than a little embarrassed by the way he had lost his temper with his father. "What I said wasn't called for 'n I apologize. Pa, I don't want ta die, nobody does, but sometime in my life I'm gonna have ta stand up like the man ya want me ta be. Ya always warned me 'bout not startin' a fight, but that I wasn't ta run from one when I was in the right. I'm in the right 'bout this here 'n, 'less ya tell me outright that I can't join up, then my mind's made up. The shootin' ain't started 'n maybe them politicians will over-rule ol' beanpole Lincoln 'n it won't come ta a war."

Lorenzo half smiled at his son's suggestion. "I been hopin' that very thing for the past thirty years, or better. Ya know son, when ya make adobe ya can only pour so much dirt inta the mud 'fore it won't mix no more. Them politicians have throwed so much dirt inta the pot, that there ain't no separatin' the good adobe from the bad dirt. It's not just y'all that worries me. I know that when war does come, it ain't gonna be over in a day or two. It'll go on for years 'n that means it'll take the twins 'n probably Tim too." Getting up from his chair, Lorenzo walked to the cupboard beneath the drain board and took out his jug of corn liquor. Pouring two cups half full, he handed one to Chet. "I know this ain't nothin' new ta ya, 'cause I smelled it on ya a couple 'a times. If your mind's made up 'bout goin' ta war, then that's the last word on it 'n may the good Lord watch over ya."

Flattered, that his father thought him enough of a man that he would share a drink with him; Chet raised his cup in a toast. "To the Confederate States of America 'n a quick end ta the war. How's that for a toast, huh Pa?"

"Not too bad, son, but can I add a bit? Here's ta a quick 'n a just end ta the war 'n soon the nation 'll be whole again." Raising the cups to their lips both drank to the toast, however deep down each knew it was only a futile dream.

CHAPTER TWO.

In faded gold script the weathered wooden sign, which hung over the front porch, read "Henry Adams Esq.". Below that, "Attorney At Law," proudly announced the office of the leading, and only, attorney in Martindale, Pennsylvania. Inside, surrounding a huge walnut desk sat three people. In a high-backed leather chair, facing those assembled, sat Mister Adams himself. The thinning gray hair, narrow rectangular spectacles, rather bulbous nose and round rosy cheeks reminded Constance Garner of her idea of Santa Claus, but without the white beard. At a mere eighteen years of age it really didn't seem that long ago, when she lay awake on Christmas Eve to see if she could hear the reindeer on the roof of her home. A woman, well past middle age, and a very elderly man made up the rest of the trio in front of the desk.

"I believe everyone concerned is present, so we will have the reading of the will," Adam's voice broke the silence. "As you are well aware we are here to read the Last Will and Testament of one, Hamblin Garner. For the record I will date this reading on the seventh day of March, eighteen hundred and sixty one. According to the instructions set by this will, you have each signed a paper guaranteeing that under no circumstances will you contest this will. They are legal and binding documents, which I will now make a part of the will." Peering over the top of his spectacles he paused, as if waiting for a comment from those seated. When none was forthcoming he opened the seal on the pile of papers before him. In a loud voice he began to read.

"I Hamblin Garner of Cyprus Wood Plantation, Rome, Georgia, leave to my abolitionist sister, Phoebe Doan and her shiftless husband Ned Doan, not one blamed cent. Instead I leave them a team of sorrel mules. Every time I hear these jackasses bray, the sound reminds me of my sister Phoebe. To each of the mules I have deposited one thousand dollars in the bank, to be used for their care and feeding, but only as long as they are alive and well cared for. The interest from the money will belong to Phoebe to use as she sees fit. However, if something should happen to either or both of the mules, the money forfeits to my brother Clarence and Phoebe gets nothing more. She had not much good to say about me in life, and probably less good to say about me now. You had best take good care of these mules little sister, for without them you don't get a penny. Mister Adams will have the welfare of this team carefully monitored."

Henry Adams paused and looked in the direction of the woman sitting to the left of Constance. Her face was a mixture of disappointment and fury as his words found their mark. "To my brother Clarence Garner, I leave three thousand dollars from my bank account. I hope he enjoys the women, whiskey and anything else he wants before he dies too, which shouldn't be too long."

Again Adams paused as he looked at the elderly man. "That much living will kill him sure," he thought to himself. "Before I go any farther I want to explain to all of you, that this will is incontestable. It is stipulated that should anyone attempt to contest the will, their portion of the settlement is to be divided between the other survivors. Now I have made that particular portion of the will clear, we shall continue." Clearing his throat and adjusting his reading glasses, Mister Adams Esquire read on.

"To Constance Garner, the only remaining child of my youngest brother, Edgar Garner, I leave the bulk of my estate. The Cyprus Wood Plantation, of which four hundred acres are in cotton and another four hundred acres yet to be developed, belong to her. The home, the animals and everything on that property also belong to Connie. At the writing of this will there are seventy-seven slaves also belonging to her." Mister Adams took the better part of an hour reading the name, age, sex, abilities and genealogy of each individual slave. "It is entirely hers to do with as she sees fit. The only stipulation is, that she must live on the grounds of Cyprus Wood for one full year before she can sell any or all of it, except for the slaves of course. There is one exception to this stipulation. There have been rumblings of discontent between the northern and southern states. If war seems imminent she should dispose of all property as soon as possible, rather than lose it all. Such a decision shall be left to my trusted attorney, Mister Adams. There is sufficient money deposited in the bank in Rome, Georgia to see to her any needs or wants, for many years. My overseer, Thomas Judd, will take care of things in her absence. He has been a trusted friend for years and I have well taken care of his lifetime financial needs previously. Thomas will help Connie to adjust to plantation living and see to any needs she may have." Turning to the last page Adams paused to rest his tired eyes, and then continued again. "At the north-east corner of the plantation is a large grove of oak trees. This spot is never to be sold, developed or otherwise disturbed.

That is the burial place of my beloved wife and myself. Last, but certainly not least, to my trusted friend Henry Adams, I leave three thousand dollars and my heartfelt thanks. Signed, this sixth day of November, eighteen hundred and sixty. Hamblin Garner."

Laying the will aside the attorney drank from a water glass on the table, then looked at those assembled. "That is all there is. I will attend to the arraignments to have each of you receive your part of the inheritance and any special instruction left by Mister Garner. You will receive these in one week's time. I bid you, Good day." With no further ado he rose, handed each a copy of the will and escorted them to the door.

Connie squinted against the afternoon sun as the door closed behind her. Opening her parasol she walked down the walk toward her waiting buggy, which was now pulled in front of the gate. Alighting from his seat in the box, the driver opened the door for her to enter and took her by the arm to help her into her seat. Fingering the envelope, given her by Mister Adams, she smiled at the driver and nodded a simple, "Thank you," as he closed the latch on the door.

She hadn't seen her grandfather since she was eight years of age, but she would never forget what he looked like. Back then he had been a very handsome man, with broad shoulders and a perpetual infectious grin on his face. He was never without the broad-brimmed white straw hat, to keep the burning sun from his face. She smiled as she recalled how she would climb onto his lap and search the pockets of his vest, looking for the candy mints that were always waiting for her. She also remembered the long train rides from Martindale to Georgia and the seemingly even longer buggy ride to the plantation.

As the buggy turned down the tree-lined lane, toward the magnificent white house, her first impression of Cyprus Wood was one of awe. The carefully manicured lawn and trimmed magnolia bushes framed the opulent mansion. A setting no artist could do justice to in any painting. Jutting out over the front, forming a cover for the porch, huge pillars held up a balcony. The cut glass windows, set on either side of the doorway, accentuated the double oak door that opened into the marble-floored entryway.

When her great aunt Phoebe learned that her brother was taking his family to visit the south, she took Connie aside privately. Her description of the severe beatings that were handed out daily to all slaves, along with the starving and squalor they were forced to endure, terrified the eight-year-old girl. She had begged her parents to be left behind when they made the journey, but her pleading fell on deaf ears. She was taken aboard the train kicking and screaming, petrified at what she must witness at the other end. She had never told her mother or father why she did not want to accompany them, only that she was afraid of trains. When the black house servants met the buggy at the front drive, Connie was amazed to see that all the women were neatly dressed in washed and ironed cotton dresses. The men servants wore white shirts and tailored trousers that would have rivaled the fashions up north.

Her grandmother was a true representative of Southern aristocracy. When she met them, as they entered the foyer, was the first time Connie had seen her. Her dress was immaculate and not a hair out of place as she glided towards them. A folded fan swung from a string on her wrist and the folded lace handkerchief, clutched in her other hand, seemed a bit ostentatious to the eight-year-old. It took but a few minutes for Connie to completely fall in love with her grandmother, who appeared to be everything that the young girl wished to be when she grew up.

For the first few days Connie was rather aloof with her grandparents and, rather than join the rest in the jaunts to see the plantation, stayed alone in her room. She had no wish to see the beatings inflicted on the defenseless blacks, or the inhumane conditions under which they were forced to exist. While the house servants dressed nice and seemed to receive decent treatment, they weren't the common field hands. Her young mind formed visions of the overseer. She pictured him wielding the long whip and using it on the backs of any of the poor unfortunates who didn't move fast enough. She was aware that Aunt Phoebe was an abolitionist and, after listening to her description of the conditions in the south, she was ready to join the cause also.

"Come on Connie," her father said as he opened the door to her room. "The rest of us are going on a picnic and you have hardly left your room since we arrived." The dreaded day had arrived at last and she must now face the truth of the terrible South. No longer could she hide in the confines of the bedroom. Procrastinating as long as possible she finally met the others on the veranda, not quite prepared to enter the bowels of Hell that was called, "Cyprus Wood Plantation."

There was no doubt that her father was grandpa's offspring. The facial structure, broad shoulders and sandy hair was nearly a mirror image of each other. Born in Philadelphia, her grandfather was the second born of the three children. Grandpa had met her grandmother at a social function for the governor of Pennsylvania.

She was visiting her relatives in Philadelphia and was to return to her home in Georgia the next day. It was love at first sight and the two danced every dance together, and then took a buggy ride around the city. By the time he returned her home, he knew this was the girl he would marry. He managed to convince her to stay a few days longer. The few days stretched into weeks, then months, as they fell deeper in love and began to make marriage plans. The letters from her parents came more often and became more demanding for her to leave Hamblin and return home immediately.

They were horrified that their daughter could possibly love, and maybe even wed, a Yankee abolitionist. The begging and threats went unheeded and grandpa's family friend, former President of the United States, John Adams, married the two in a quiet ceremony. The next week they left for her home to face her hostile parents. It didn't take long for Hamblin to win her mother and father over. Before his beloved wife Anna passed away, the lovers spent nearly fifty years together,.

"Are you enjoying the ride, Connie?" Her grandfather's voice brought her back to reality. She had been looking but not really seeing the tree-lined lane, as they drove toward the vast expanse of cotton plants that covered as far as she could see. Like so many ants the rows were filled with blacks, each dragging a long sack behind them as they picked the boles of the plants clean and filled the bags. This was Connie's first exposure to any slaves and she was surprised to find the absence of the brutality that she had been warned about. The voices coming from the fields were raised in a chanting kind of song as they moved from plant to plant. Stopping the surrey before one of the men, Hamblin called the man over to him.

"Yes Masta Garner," the beckoned one said, as he approached the surrey. "What can ol' Moses do for the Masta? We'uns got nearly this section picked 'n gonna start on th' next one right soon now." Connie was surprised to see the lack of welts or scars on the naked back, which Phoebe had assured her all slaves bore. Perhaps this was only an isolated case. She was certain that a person who attended church every Sunday, like Aunt Phoebe did, wouldn't lie to her.

Climbing down from the seat, Hamblin invited the rest to join him. "Come with me and I'll show you how we grow cotton. Just be careful, 'cause these boles have sharp points on 'em 'n they can cut a body pretty good. When the field hands first start we give 'em pads to wear on their fingers, 'til they get tough enough to keep from getting' stuck." Leading the way down the rows, he explained the intricacies of raising a bumper crop of cotton. As they passed the field hands, Hamblin called each by name and received a polite greeting in return.

"He puts on a pretty good act," Connie thought to herself, as she held her skirt away from the plants. "The man with the whip is no doubt hiding until we go away, then he will rein terror upon these poor souls." Looking at the backs of each slave, as they walked slowly through the maze of pickers, she saw not one single case of any abuse. "Grandpa," her inquisitiveness finally getting the better of her, "where are the ones that you have to whip?"

An astonished look replaced the smile on Hamblin Garner's

face. "Whip? You won't find a whip on all of Cyprus Wood. While these folks are my property, same as my home 'n that surrey, they still feel pain 'n bleed same as you 'n me. I never held with whippin' no man 'n I don't intend to start. If I have a problem with one of the blacks, I sell him off. When you start whippin' a body to make them submit, all that happens is you fuel hates 'n not respect. These people are treated well, fed well and have a decent place to live. You won't find one scarred back on this whole place."

She recalled how her grandmother had knelt before her; mindless of the dirt that was soiling her satin dress. Holding Connie close to her bosom, she told her of the way life had always been at Cyprus Wood Plantation. "When your grandpa and I first came here this was little more than a swamp, a bunch of trees and brush.

The land was virtually worthless, so your grandpa sold everything he had amassed all of his life and we bought it. We had two mules and a borrowed plow to our names. The two of us would work side by side from sunup to sundown, just to clear the ground and drain the swamp. Many a night we'd be too tired 'n sore to sleep. It took us nearly four years to clear enough to plant our first crop. All that time we lived in a clapboard shack that had only one room. The demand for cotton grew and so did the land we cleared.

When the cotton gin came along the demand for cotton couldn't keep up with the supply. Grandpa mortgaged the place 'n we bought our first three blacks. We have never looked upon any of them as slaves, but rather investments that we need to take care of in order to make the place grow. Time passed and we did grow into one of the largest cotton plantations in the south. Without the foresight and hard work of your grandfather, none of this could ever have happened. I don't know where you got the idea that we whip slaves here, but very few of the plantation owners do. That would be the same as beating an expensive horse to make it mind. Most of the good field hands we paid a high price for, and we can't take the chance of injuring them by beating them. Instead we treat them with kindness and are rewarded rather than hated. When we go to bed at night we never have to worry about a slave uprising, that may end in our being murdered in our sleep. I doubt there is one person in these fields that wouldn't give their life for your grandfather."

"We're here ma'am," the voice of the footman brought Connie out of her reverie. Stepping from the carriage, she thanked the man and walked up the four steps to her door. Turning the key in the latch, she gently pushed the door open. The smell of fresh baked pies greeted her as she walked toward the kitchen.

"Well my dear, how did things go at the attorney's office?" A woman in her late fifties met Connie as she passed through the door and sat at the table. "Here's a piece of fresh apple pie and there's milk in the crock. Tell me all about what happened."

Ida Kramer had been the housekeeper for the Garners for the past twenty years. She was present when Connie saw the first light of day and looked upon the girl as her own. When both of Connie's parents were killed in a runaway buggy accident two years ago, it was Mrs. Kramer who had never left her side since that day. The couple were returning home from a party in a two-wheel buggy pulled by a single horse. A bolt of lightning and the accompanying crack of thunder so startled the poor animal that it bolted. Try as he may there was no controlling the terrified horse. As they turned a curve in the muddy road, the edge of a wheel caught and the buggy spun wildly then tipped onto it's top. Connie still had dreams of the constable coming to the door to tell her of the demise of both parents. Taking the chair across from Connie, Ida brushed back a wild strand of hair from her face and eagerly waited for the girl to tell her all that happened. Between mouthfuls of pie Connie told all that had transpired at the office of Mister Adams.

"I really don't know what to do now. I haven't even seen Cyprus Wood in over ten years. With the slave issue so strong I'm a bit frightened. There's talk of Georgia, along with others, joining Carolina in secession. I certainly don't wish to be caught there if that happens. I know this is a lot to ask of anyone, but would you accompany me if I must go to Georgia? I have no one else to turn to and I'm too frightened to go alone."

"Child, there is no way that I would let you go without me," Mrs. Kramer answered with no hesitation. "In my opinion, there is no way that there won't be a war. Perhaps we could go to Rome, withdraw your money from the bank and have someone sell the plantation for you, then send you the proceeds. I'm sure the attorney would agree to that, rather than put you in harms way by staying there. It's too late in the day now, however tomorrow we shall return to his office and ask his advice."

Finishing the remainder of her pie, Connie went to her room and lay across the canopied bed. As much as she hated the thought of selling Cyprus Wood, other than ignoring it completely, she could see no other way. Her grandfather had entrusted her with the plantation that he had worked so hard to obtain; now she couldn't ignore her responsibility. Even if she simply emancipated the slaves and turned the place over to the overseer, she must do something. As she stared at the canopy drape over her head her thoughts returned to that day of the picnic and her tour of the plantation.

"Ham darling, I really believe that perhaps we should delay the picnic for a bit and show our guests the rest of Cyprus Wood. It may dispel some of the misconceptions that Connie seems to have about us." As they returned to the carriage her grandmother had pulled her close. "Don't worry little one. We Southerners are not the ogres that some have painted us as being. Once you get to know us we appear to be almost human."

The ride was a bumpy one as they wound through row after row of long dwellings. The exteriors of all were whitewashed, while the doors stood open to catch the slightest hint of a breeze. "These are where the single bucks live and clear over the other side the single females. This section here's for couples and those with families. We don't allow any mixing of single men and women, that's your grandma's idea." An innocent eight-year-old, Connie had to ask why? She smiled now as she remembered how red grandpa's face had gotten at her inquisitiveness. "Grandma will tell you later," he mumbled as he hastened the horses into a trot, in a hurry to leave that part of the tour behind quickly.

"We have over seventy slaves on this plantation and every one of them is worth upwards of five hundred dollars or more. Since Mister Whitney came up with the cotton gin, the demand for cotton has grown out of proportion to what can be raised. Along with that demand for cotton, the demand for slaves to work the fields has also grown. The number of slaves brought in has doubled, or even tripled, in the past few years. For the first time, the south is seeing prosperity knocking its door down and those busybodies up north are trying to strangle us. Most of the slaves we have here are from our own stock, but there are a few that were bought. Moses there came from a plantation that gave up raising crops and went to raising nothing but Blacks for the markets. They keep records on every male and female on the place. By selective breeding they turn out a crop of slaves that brings in more money than all the cotton they could raise."

"Breeding is hardly a subject for the tender ears of your lady companions," his wife interrupted Ham. "Perhaps we should continue the tour." Quickly changing the subject, Anna then explained that there was no work on the Sabbath or Christmas Day. Those days belonged to the Lord and Christian church services were held for those wishing to attend.

"You paint a pretty picture Ham, but certainly there must be problems with the slaves. What happens if one of them rebels, or tries to run away? What happens to them then?" His sister-in-law asked. "I'm sure this can't all be so serine."

"Like any society we have our problems. As for running, we have only had a handful ever try to run. Most came back on their own and a few were captured and returned to us. Only two never returned and we never heard of what happened to one of them. A plantation owner down the way shot the other when the fellow tried to break into his storeroom. If they run they're put into the box for seven days. It's five feet long three feet wide and five feet high.

There are no windows and it's totally dark inside. For the first two days they receive neither food nor water, after that there is only enough of each given to sustain life. It sounds barbaric but no more so than some of the prisons up north. Usually the box cures them of ever running again, but if they do I sell them off. At the far end is our own version of a jail. As of now there is only one occupant. I found him guilty of beating his black overseer with a hoe and I sentenced him to hang. He was supposed to hang today, however I postponed the execution until after you folks leave." Connie was startled at the matter-of-fact way her grandfather talked of hanging another man. Three days later they left for home and she often wondered if Ham actually did hang the slave?

It was dark now and she still lay there thinking of the past and of the uncertain future, when there was a rap on her bedroom door. "Honey, Mister Adams is here to see you," Mrs. Kramer called from the other side. "There is a matter that he must discuss with you."

"Thank you, Mrs. Kramer. Please tell him that I shall be there immediately." Fumbling to light the lamp, Connie finally managed to put a match to the wick. Holding the lamp before her she entered the living room and greeted the man whose office she had visited that very afternoon. "This is a pleasant surprise. I hadn't expected to see you for another week. I hope there isn't a problem." Sitting across from the elderly attorney she waited for an answer.

"There may be an insurmountable problem. As you are well aware, there are rumblings of a war between the States and there lies the problem. I have the authority to nullify the stipulation that requires you to live at Cyprus Wood for the year's time. Due to the conditions that are facing the nation, I have drawn up a paper that releases you from that stipulation. You are free to dispose of the plantation in any manner that you see fit, with no threat of forfeiture on your behalf. It is my advice to sell, trade or give away that place as soon as possible. I have contacted the bank in Rome and they refuse to release a sum of money that large to anyone, unless they appear at the bank in person. Along with the release, I have placed seven hundred dollars advance in this envelope. It will take care of your tickets and expenses on the trip, should you decide to go in spite of my advice."

"I truly appreciate your concern. However, I feel that I must at least try to fulfill my grandfather's wishes," Connie said, as she placed a hand on the arm of the elderly gentleman.

"Then for your safety, you should take an able-bodied man with you for protection. If I were a younger man, I would go with you. I must recommend that you go tomorrow and buy a train ticket, get there, get the money and get home as fast as possible." So saying he stood, kissed Connie's hand and left the house.

There was to be no sleep for Connie that night. She knew of no man she could ask to accompany her on such a journey, so Mrs. Kramer would have to do. It was impossible that they could even be ready to leave by the next day. Packing, buying tickets and closing up the house, wasn't something that could be done in such a short time. A million thoughts ran through her head before the sun peeked through the curtains of her bedroom. Quietly she got dressed, as not to disturb the housekeeper's sleep. As she put her hand on the knob she heard the rattle of pans in the kitchen. Mrs. Kramer was preparing breakfast as she entered the room.

"You didn't get much sleep either, I take it," she smiled at Connie. "We're going to need a nourishing breakfast if we're going to be on the go all day. Lord knows if we'll have another chance to eat." Connie had never been one who could stand the thought of food so early in the day. As far back as she could remember, the housekeeper had insisted that breakfast was the most nourishing meal of the day. More than once the two had butted heads over whether Connie was to eat or not. The stack of hotcakes and plate of scrambled eggs were the last things that Connie wanted to see.

"My stomach is churning too badly to try to eat," she said as she sat at the table. "Just a cup of black coffee will do me fine." She knew the inevitable argument was coming, but she stuck with her excuse for not eating. Two cups of coffee and the usual lecture on proper eating habits later, they retired to their separate rooms to dress for the day's exhausting schedule.

First on the agenda was to buy the tickets and arrange for a compartment on the train. They wanted a secluded room, where they needn't worry about two women traveling alone being molested by common riff-raff. The only train to Georgia left in two hours and there was no way they could make that one, so they purchased tickets on the one leaving the following morning. Next came the endless shopping for the many personal items that are so vital on such a long journey. The hair parlor took most of the day, and it was near sundown by the time they mounted the steps of home. Both women were exhausted from no sleep the previous night and the busy day's events.

"It looks like we'll both sleep sitting up in a chair tonight," Mrs. Kramer laughed as she dropped into the overstuffed chair. "It's either that, or we wasted good money on these hairdos. Putting fancy hair on this old body's like painting the side of a barn. It may improve the looks, but underneath there's still the same old cracked boards." Connie giggled at the analogy. Sitting on the arm of the chair, Connie took the older woman by the hand.

"You dear sweet person, I don't know what I would do without you. Mister Adams seems to think there is an element of risk associated with this trip. In no way do I want to place you in any danger, so I'm asking you to please stay here and I will go alone." The reaction was as she had expected.

"You must be loony, if you think I'd let you go by yourself," Mrs. Kramer exploded. "Do you think for a moment that I've babied you all these years, only to let you go off to such a place by yourself now? Not on your mother's corset are you leaving me behind. I've been in this household too many years to let you slip through my fingers now. I don't want to hear another word about it. Is that clear, young lady?"

"I understand," Connie replied softly. "It would have always bothered me if I hadn't given you a chance to back out. Believe me, I was praying that you would do just as you have and not decided to stay behind. To be very honest with you, I'm terrified of what's ahead and I need someone like you for support." They sat holding each other for a while before parting for the night.

The two women were working on their second cup of coffee when enough daylight filtered through the window to turn out the oil lamp on the table. They had been up for over an hour and with six hours before train time; they made plans for the trip south. Ida Kramer had packed and unpacked the picnic basket three times and was in the process of doing it again.

"Cold meat sandwiches, fried chicken, a jar of mustard pickles with lots of those little onions that you like so much, napkins, a slab of cheese and a loaf of bread. I know that I'm forgetting something but for the life of me, I can't think of what it is. Do you know of anything else we need in here, Connie?"

Absorbed in thought the girl had been staring at the dregs in the bottom of her cup. Her mind was a thousand miles away at a plantation, which she now owned and the decisions that she must make. Some of the problems seemed insurmountable, especially when she had no control over them. It had even occurred to her to forget the whole matter and stay home. After all, she had managed to live modestly on the money left her by the estate of her parents. If she was especially frugal the money should last another two years or so.

"I'm sorry Mrs. Kramer, were you talking to me?" Connie asked as she brought her eyes from the cup to the housekeeper's face. "I was just wondering if we are really doing the right thing by leaving here? I suppose there are always doubts when one faces the unknown. Perhaps I'm just dreading that long train ride."

"I've been thinking. Maybe you should call me, 'Aunt Ida,' instead of 'Mrs. Kramer.' We may be a bit safer if folks think you're my niece, especially when some man wants to flirt with you. With those kinds an aunt carries a lot more clout than a plain house-keeper does. As pretty as you are, I'm going to have my hands full just chasing off the men anyway and every bit of leverage helps.'"

"Aunt Ida it is. You were always more than a housekeeper to me anyhow. Perhaps I should have started calling you that years ago. Do you really believe that there is any danger of us being bothered by strange men?" A look of concern wrinkled Connie's forehead, "I mean really bother us? I've had fellows flirt with me before and one or two try to get fresh, but never really try to take advantage of me."

"Honey, with a face as pretty as yours and a shape like you have, it's bound to happen sooner or later. As saggy as my body is, along with a face that would crack a mirror, there's no danger of any man chasing me. It's you I have to look out for and as long as I have this I won't worry as much." Reaching into the folds of the basket, she produced a tiny derringer pistol. "This belonged to my late husband. It's been gathering dust in my drawer all these years and now it may come in handy. To tell you the truth, I've never even shot this thing. I'm deathly afraid of any kind of firearm. I figure that any shaky old dame pointing this at a man may not change his mind, but it'll sure make him think twice about doing anything silly." Replacing the pistol back into the folds she resumed rum-maging through the basket. "I sure wish I could think of what's missing in here."

"Is there a knife to slice the bread and cheese? I don't recall you mentioning that," Connie volunteered. "We may also need some-thing to get the pickles out of the jar with."

"That's what's missing, silver. It's a good thing you're thinking or we'd really be in a mess." Placing a handful of silverware into the basket Ida closed the lid. "One more cup of coffee and we'd best get ready to leave for the train station. I'd much rather be an hour early than one minute late." Connie agreed and they made small talk over the last of the brew, and then went to double check their luggage.

The platform was crowded when the two arrived and they gave their baggage to a porter inside the depot. No sooner had they stepped out of the office than the puffing of the ancient steam engine could be heard in the distance. A cloud of black smoke announced it's location, as it drew nearer to town, and before long the engine pulled even with the platform. A jet of steam was expelled and the conductor stepped down from one of the cars. Ida and Connie hurried toward him and gave him their tickets.

"Drawing room C, fourth car down," he mumbled as he indicated the direction they should go, with a jerk of his head. "The porter will show you to your accommodations." Eyeing the stuffed picnic basket, he added with a note of sarcasm, "I was going to mention that there's no room service on this run and if you want food, there's car serving sandwiches. From the looks of it, you have enough there to last all the way to Georgia."

Ida matched his sarcasm with a curt, "Thanks," and the two walked to their car and boarded. The room was small but acceptable. A two-teared bunk folded against one side, while a tiny table, two chairs and a washbasin occupied the other. This was to be home for the next several days. After a longer than expected wait, the engine gained steam and the train jerked into motion. As the depot slowly passed the window Connie sighed.

"Well Aunt Ida, it's too late for you to back out now, unless you plan to jump from a moving train that is. I only hope we aren't getting into something we'll be sorry for later. I guess it's all in the hands of the good Lord now. There isn't much we mere mortals can do to change things. Not much at all."

CHAPTER THREE.

"Who can that be knockin' at the door this time 'a day?" Samantha Baxter mumbled, as she shook the excess flour from her hands and wiped them on her pinafore apron. " Seems like everyone knows it's bakin' day 'n that's the time they got ta come 'n visit." Shaking her head in disgust she pulled the door open.

"Surprise Ma," Chet grinned, as he stood ramrod stiff and snapped a smart salute to his mother. "How do ya like my new duds? Pretty fancy 'n they prett' near fit too. Needs a bit 'a takin' up in the legs 'n the sleeves is a bit long. But ten minutes with a needle 'n thread 'n you'll have me a spankin' uniform."

The sight of her son, dressed in the gray trimmed with yellow uniform of the Confederacy, did not exactly thrill her. Both she and her husband had scrimped, and often gone without their own necessities, just so the boys could have a few of the nicer things. It was difficult for her to admit that Chet was no longer a child and it was time for her to cut the apron strings. Pa had told her that same thing time after time, but it's different feelings that a mother has for her offspring. Men never felt the baby kicking inside the womb, nor experienced the pain of childbirth. Pa usually slept all the times she sat in the chair nights and nursed the infant, strengthening the bond that only exists between a mother and child. Severing these ties was not as easy as cutting the umbilicus, for it goes much deeper than that.

"Ten minutes, is it?" Ma said, as she turned away, afraid that he would see the tears forming in her eyes. "It'll take the best part 'a the night ta get that ta fit ya. Come on in, your lettin' every fly in the county in 'n I got bread bakin'." Wiping her face with the corner of her apron, she returned to her dough.

"Is that all you got ta say 'bout my new uniform? Ya should 'a seen the looks I got from the folks downtown. I sashayed down the street 'n boy, did I get the whistles from the gals." Chet got his hand slapped as he picked a piece of dough and popped it into his mouth. "Now y'all wouldn't deny the newest member 'a Missouri's Eighth a little bite 'a dough, would ya Ma?"

"I'd smack Jeff Davis his self if he was a reachin' inta my vittles. New soldier or old, it makes no never mind ta me, I still run this here kitchen. Now back off a ways 'fore ya get flour all over your pretty outfit 'n I gotta clean it, on top 'a everythin' else I gotta do." Kneading the flour into the dough she smiled at the thought of her actually smacking ol' Jeff Davis.

As if Chet read her thoughts he laughed. "I think you'd get shot as a traitor if ya really hit Jeff Davis. 'sides, he ain't as fast as I am." Dodging the swipe at his thieving hand, another piece of dough was swept into his mouth. "Ya know Ma? I don't know which I'm gonna miss more, your home cookin' or Pa's yarns 'bout the ol' days. One thing certain, I hope the Yankees all aim as bad as y'all, 'cause ya ain't hit me yet," as he reached for another spot of bread dough. This time he received a severe whack on the knuckles with the wooden spoon that Ma held ready.

"I doubt it'll be neither one. It ain't my cookin' or Pa's yarns that keep ya out half the night, more like some blond-haired gal in town. Far as them Yankee's aim goes, ya best hope that their rifles misfire as much as your mouth does." Looking out the kitchen window Ma smiled, "If ya want ta surprise your brothers with your new duds, ya best hide 'cause they're turnin' down the lane. Just like always them twins is pickin' on Timothy."

Rubbing his bruised knuckles, Chet stood behind the door just as it opened and all three boys tried to get through it at the same time. Naturally it was Tim who got pushed away, while Chad and Tad pushed their way in. As the little brother came inside he was grabbed from behind in a bear hug that made him screech loudly.

"Now I got y'all, ya Yankee spy 'n I'm gonna whisker burn ya ta death." Tim gave out with a loud screech, as Chet lifted him off the floor and tried to get his chin against the wiggling boy's cheek.

"I ain't no Yankee spy, ya dimwit. I'm Jeff Davis 'n I'll bust ya one if ya don't put me down," Tim giggled. "Some soldier your gonna make. Can't tell ol' Jeff from some ol' Yankee spy. Hope the rest 'a the army sees better than y'all, or they'll end up shootin' Stonewall Jackson by mistake."

"Can't nobody shoot ol' Stonewall Jackson, why do ya think they call him, 'Stonewall?' I bet it's cause the minnie balls 'll bounce right off 'n him," Chad grinned, as he tried to grab hold of Tim's feet. All he got for his efforts was a well-placed kick in the chest that sent him sprawling.

"All right, you roughnecks," Ma hollered, as the wrestling was getting out of hand. "There ain't no horse-play in the house. Chet, y'all put Tim down 'n twins, ya get your chores done 'fore Pa gets home. I 'bout got the bread done 'n got no time for these shenanigans."

With both feet safely on the floor, Tim turned to face his elder brother. "Boy Chet, ya sure do look sharp in that there uniform. Don't ya think he looks sharp, Ma? Do ya reckon I could try on your coat? I promise I won't spill or nothin' on it." His eyes fairly sparkled as he admired the heavy coat and trousers.

"Ya he looks sharp, okay," Ma agreed, as she brushed back an errant lock of hair from her face, "but under all that fancy clothes it's still Chet. "Now get 'em off 'n put on your work duds. There's wood ta chop 'n clinkers ta haul out. Just 'cause the whole world's gone crazy don't mean we got ta give up chores here. Maybe if them politicians had more work 'n less time on their hands, the country wouldn't be in the shape it is now."

The boys climbed the stairs to the loft, leaving Ma to her own chores and thoughts. She still couldn't accept the fact that her little Chester was now a Confederate soldier. Tomorrow, the next day or next month, eventually he would leave home to fight the inevitable war. Tears again formed in the tired eyes as she thought of the dreaded day to come. She had never had an easy life and was certain that she would be able to face any situation as it arose.

How would she face this particular one? She had never sent a son off to war with the prospects of never seeing him again. The strains of, "Dixie," being whistled by her sons, drifted down through the ceiling. Samantha Baxter buried her face in her arms and sobbed silently.

Upstairs Chet regaled the younger lads with made-up stories

of how the war would be fought and the certain Southern victory. "Why we'll have them Blue-Bellies on the run so fast, that I'll probably be home for supper the same day I leave. I don't see the whole thing takin' more than a couple 'a hours." Each one tried on the gray coat and wished that they were the ones who were fortunate enough to wear such a grand item.

"Just look at the yellow trim on them sleeves," Tad exclaimed as he slipped his arms into the sleeves. "The Confederates sure picked a better color than that ol' blue of the North's. How's 'bout lettin' me try on that cap too? Kind 'a like that there decoration in the front." Chet handed him the cap and Tad ran his fingers over the gold lettering on the large emblem. "CSA," he read proudly, "Confederate States America."

"Confederate States OF America," Chet corrected Tad. "You done left out the, 'OF.' I reckon they leave the, 'O' out 'cause it's such a little word. We best get our duds changed 'fore Ma yells for us. Pa ought 'ta be home in a few hours 'n I can hardly wait ta see the look on his face when he sees me in this fancy get-up.'"

Having cried herself out, Samantha wiped her red eyes with her handkerchief, which was always present in the pocket of her apron. Just as she thought that there was not a tear left in her, more sobs would rack her narrow frame and she would bury her face once again to keep from being heard by those directly above her.

"Ma," came Tad's voice from the loft, "smells like your bread's burnin'." Jumping to her feet she pulled down the oven door. Plumes of smoke filled the kitchen as she pulled the charcoal remains of the afternoon's labor from the stove. Opening the front door she waved her apron in an attempt to clear some of the smoke from the room. Soon the boys joined her and each was frantically waving flour sack dishtowels toward the open door.

"Don't cry Ma," Tim said as he looked into his mother's face, "we can cut off the burned part 'n nobody 'll know the difference." The twins used their cloths and carried the still smoldering loaves outside.

"That shows how dumb ya are," Chad scoffed at Tim's statement. "Ya couldn't cut off the burned parts 'a them with an ax. They's as hard as an adobe brick."

Ignoring his brother's sarcasm, Tim was still attempting to console his mother. "Please don't cry," he pleaded, his own eyes began to water in sympathy. "It'll be okay. We didn't want no bread tonight anyhow."

Patting her youngster on top of his head, Samantha smiled down at him. "Now don't y'all get all upset, I ain't cryin'. I just got some smoke in my eyes when I opened the oven door," she lied. "We still got four loaves coolin' on the table. That's what I get for tryin' ta do too many things at once. Let's get the chores done 'fore Pa gets home 'n after supper there's huckleberry pie for dessert."

The sound of a horse being pushed hard interrupted the conversation. The younger boys fought for a spot at the window while Chet and his mother went to the door. A man in the uniform of the Confederacy rode his lathered horse down the lane and stopped before the house.

"It's Keith Staten," Chet said excitedly, "he's one 'a the officers in the Missouri Eighth. He's sure ridin' that horse inta the ground. Wonder what's so all-fire important that a body'd treat an animal that way?" Reining the stumbling horse to a fast halt before the cabin, Staten vaulted to the ground. His breath came in short gasps as he took the steps two at a time.

"Ya best pack up Chet, our outfit has done been called up. We're movin' out tonight ta back up some fellas closer ta the Mason-Dixon line. Ya got two hours ta be by the bandstand, at the Town Square, 'n ready ta leave." He was about to turn to leave when Samantha stopped him.

"Back up some fellas for what? There ain't no shootin' war goin' on, least ways none that I heard of. 'sides, he can't leave that soon. His Pa won't be home 'til after that 'n ya can't expect him ta go off without seein' his Pa first. It ain't Christian not ta let him say his, 'Good-byes.' Can't he stay 'til tomorrow, he only joined up yesterday?'"

"Sorry Miz Baxter," the young officer apologized, "by tomorrow we'll all be on a train bound for the east. I know how hard it is ta leave your loved ones. I had ta say, 'Goodbye', ta my wife 'n baby, but we're soldiers now 'n devotion ta the country comes first. I understand your feelin's, I really do. I know it ain't much comfort ta ya, but there's gonna be thousands of mothers who feel just like y'all do."

"Ya wouldn't want me ta shirk my duty, would ya Ma?" Chet took up the cause. "There ain't nothin' nobody can do now but pray that this'll all be over soon, 'n we can come home ta our loved ones." Goodbye was inevitable and tears formed in the eyes of everyone in the Baxter family. Hugging his mother, Chet looked over her shoulder at the officer. "I'll be at the square soon as I can get there. I ain't even been issued a rifle yet. What do I do 'bout that?"

Turning in the saddle Keith shouted, as he set the spurs to his horse. "That'll all be taken care of at the station. They's packin' crates 'a new rifles 'n cartridges on the cars right now. You'll get one 'a them spankin new Springfields." The rest of what he said was lost in the thunder of hooves as he galloped away.

"Tad, y'all get on the mare 'n ride ta your Pa. Tell him what's happened 'n y'all 'n him meet us at the square. No sense him comin' clear home 'n takin' a chance on missin' Chet." Drying her eyes once more Ma issued orders in a manner that would make any general envious. While Tad saddled the horse, Chad and Tim were busy setting the table. "Can't have no son 'a mine leavin' on a empty stomach," Ma said over Chet's protests that there wasn't time to eat. Under her watchful eye Chet packed the bare necessities into a small ditty bag. Satisfied that he had sufficient clean underwear and socks, along with the rest, she left the loft to supervise the kitchen duty. Soon the smell of frying potatoes, onions and pork wafted through the cracks in the floor.

Alone for the first time, Chet knelt beside his bed folded his hands and offered a silent prayer. "Lord, I been prayin' ta Ya long as I can remember. Most 'a the time it was for somethin' silly, like makin' the catfish bite or that I could shoot me a deer, stuff like that. Now I got a real favor ta ask 'a Ya. Please watch over my family while I'm gone 'n take special good care 'a them. Don't let no harm come ta nobody, 'n watch over me so's nothin' bad 'll happen ta me neither. I know there's gonna be a whole lot 'a other folks askin' Ya for the same favors. You're gonna be right down busy, but I'd sure appreciate it if Y'all could see Your way clear ta grant me this one boon. I'm a thankin' Ya now Lord for all You've done for us, 'n for the family that Ya gave ta me. Amen." Standing up he brushed the knees of the new uniform, ran a comb through his hair and slowly walked down the loft stairs for the last time before leaving home. Pausing with his hand on the bottom of the railing, Private Chester Baxter posed proudly. "Well Ma, what do ya think 'a your soldier boy now?"

"Handsome, very handsome," came the reply. "I'm just sorry that I didn't have that ten minutes ta make them pants fit better. Maybe y'all can find one 'a them southern bells ta sew them for ya. Good-lookin' fella like y'all shouldn't have no problem there. Sure ta be one 'a them that knows how ta use a needle 'n thread. Now that we all have admired ya, come on 'n eat your vittles 'fore they get cold."

The meal was a silent and rather hurried event. No one dared say anything for fear that their emotions would get the better of them. Wiping up the last of the gravy, with a piece of bread, Chet pushed back his chair.

"I reckon that time's come 'n I can't put off leavin' no longer. Will ya tell Cynthia why I didn't see her 'fore I left? I never got a chance to let her see me in my new outfit. Twins, will ya hitch up the wagon 'n bring it 'round front? I got ta have a minute alone with Ma. Tim y'all can fetch my bag from the loft." When the rest had departed Chet held his mother close in a tight embrace. "Just want ta tell ya Ma, that I love ya more 'n I could ever say in words. I know I ain't always been the perfect example for the younger ones, but maybe some day I can make up for that. If I come through this safe, I got a lot of makin' up ta do ta a lot 'a folks. I'll write ya as often as I can, but if ya don't hear from me for a while, don't worry none." The embrace tightened, as each was hesitant to release the other. Tim's appearance, at about the same time Chad yelled that the wagon was ready, forced them to part. Tousling the hair of his youngest brother Chet smiled down at him. "Thanks Tim, 'n don't forget your promise ta be the man around here 'n help the folks."

Taking his bag in hand the family loaded into the wagon and drove down the dusty lane. Chet momentarily pulled the horses to a halt and after a short look behind, as if painting a mental picture to take with him, clicked his tongue and slapped the reins on the backs of the team. "It may be a long time 'fore I get ta see that place again."

Word quickly spread throughout the town and byways that the

Missouri Eighth Regiment had been called up and were leaving tonight. People lined the road and as they drove by flowers were given to Chet, while shouts from the well-wishers were heard along the way. Women waved handkerchiefs, while men doffed their hats and placed them over their hearts. An occasional handmade Confederate flag waved in the slight breeze. Chet had never felt so important in his entire life. As the wagon approached the lane leading to the Harris' farm his heart leaped, for there stood Cynthia, her father, mother and two brothers. Pulling the team to a halt he jumped from the seat, losing his hat in the process, and hugged Cynthia.

Unabashed he kissed her full on the lips, in a kiss that was a bit too long for her mother's liking.

"I was afraid that I wouldn't have a chance ta see ya 'fore I left," Chet whispered, as he held her close. "I'm gonna miss ya somethin' terrible, Cynthia. Do ya reckon your folks'd let ya go to see me off?" One of her brothers had retrieved Chet's hat and was tugging at his pants leg in an attempt to give it back. "Thanks Button, " Chet said as he replaced the hat. "Mister Harris, would it be okay if Cynthia came along? My folks'd make sure she got home safely, once the train leaves."

Cynthia's father extended his hand to Chet. "I don't have no problem with that, long as your folks 'll be there too. Goodbye Chet, 'n you take care not ta get yourself hurt, ya hear? We got big plans for y'all 'n little Cynthia when ya get back." The last comment drew him a nudge in the ribs and a sour look from his wife. "Ya best be gettin', I hear that there train's leavin' right soon." Helping his daughter into the seat, they waved as the wagon disappeared down the road.

For Chet and Cynthia the ride into town was not nearly long enough. They had so much more to say to each other as they turned into the square, which was lined with horses, wagons and buggies of all descriptions. Men in uniform milled about, most with young ladies hanging onto their arms. The din reminded Tim of a hive of angry bees. As more joined the already overcrowded square the volume increased, until Tim finally put his fingers in his ears to shut out some of the noise. Standing on the wagon seat he strained to find Pa and Tad in the sea of humanity, but it was like looking for a particular snowflake in the midst of a blizzard.

"Pa ain't never gonna find us in all these folks," he shouted to his mother. "I can't even see the mare nowhere. Maybe Tad never found Pa 'n he'll miss seein' Chet 'fore he goes." Ma either didn't hear him in the commotion, or was flat ignoring him. Standing on his tiptoes he resumed his search for any sign of the rest of his family.

The sudden report of a rifle fired in the center of the square made the horses lurch in surprise, nearly dumping Tim out of the back of the box.

"Missouri Eighth Regiment, fall in," the order from the officer in charge was echoed by the subordinate officers and noncoms. What had seemed to be mass confusion one minute became a deafening silence the next. Final hugs and kisses were exchanged, as the troops slowly pulled away from the ones they would be leaving behind. Chad and Ma had stood a respectful distance from Chet and Cynthia, to let them have their good-byes, but now Ma threw her arms around her son's neck.

"I've never told ya enough how much ya mean ta Pa 'n me. I reckon we never even thought about the day when ya wouldn't be around the house no more." Her voice wavered as she clung to her eldest son. "We had such big plans for the four 'a ya boys. Ta see ya married 'n ta bounce your little ones on our knees, 'n watch ya make somethin' 'a your lives."

"Shucks Ma, you're just seein' me off on a trip, not plantin' me in the ground. I'll be back 'fore ya know it 'n maybe then me 'n Cynthia can start on them little ones your lookin' forward ta so much." Chet grinned at the prospect; while Cynthia's face turned the brightest red that he had ever seen her blush. " Not 'til after we get properly married," he was quick to add. "I reckon that I best get 'fore they shoot me for bein' a deserter already." Pulling away from his mother he started to shake hands with Chad, but when he noticed the tears running down the tan cheeks suddenly embraced him instead. "We ain't never gonna get too old ta give each other a bear hug, now are we boy?" Not to be left out of the goodbye Tim clung to Chet's leg. Dropping to one knee Chet hugged the youngest member of the family. "Remember, ya got 'ta be the man now. Look after the rest 'n I'll be home soon ta spell ya."

"Chet," Cynthia's soft voice brought him to his feet, "keep this near you, just to remind you that I will be waiting for you to come home." Reaching behind her neck she undid the clasp on a small heart necklace and put it in the pocket of his jacket. A lingering kiss and Private Baxter pulled away and, with a wave over his shoulder, hurried to join those already in line.

"Chet. Chet Baxter," a voice carried over the rest. Turning he saw Pa and Tad, on a dead run toward him, cutting across the lawn of the square. "We was afraid we'd miss ya in this mess," Pa said as he tried to catch his breath. "I know ya ain't got no time ta gab, so I'll say what I got ta say quick. I love ya boy, 'n I'd do anythin' if I could go in your place. I know I ain't always been the Pa ya could be proud 'a, but we all got short-comin's. I just got a few more 'en most folks. Take care 'a yourself 'n come home soon."

"Get one 'a them Blue-Bellies for me, Chet. Give 'em what for, just for startin' this thing in the first place. I hate 'em, I hate 'em all." Tad held his brother close as he sobbed the words.

"Ya mustn't feel that way, Tad. They's just doin' what they think's right, same as me. Can't hold them responsible for this here war, 'cause it was them hard-headed politicians what started this whole thing."

A hand gripping his shoulder made Chet lookup. It was Keith Staten; his face reflected his sympathy at breaking into their private moment. "Sorry folks, but ya best be gettin' on with the rest 'a the men Chet. We're movin' out ta the depot in a few minutes, soon as I round up a couple more 'a the stragglers."

With a final hug, Chet picked up his ditty bag and joined the rest in formation. Finding a place beside a youth his own age, he extended his hand to him. "Name's Baxter, Chet Baxter," he volunteered. "Don't recollect seein' ya 'round these here parts before."

"That's 'cause I ain't from these here parts, 'n I don't give a snap what your name is." The rebuke set Chet back on his heels.

"Just tryin' ta be friendly's all. Don't mean ta get your back up. Thought as long as we're travelin' together we might as well be friends." Chet felt a mixture of indignation and hurt at the treatment.

"Look fella. My Pa's been in fightin' 'fore 'n he tells me ta not make no friends. Ya got ta look after friends 'n then ya up 'n get yourself killed. Long as I don't know ya, I don't give a hang 'bout ya 'n I stay alive when the shootin' starts. If ya want a friend, find yourself another place ta stand, 'cause I ain't interested."

"You're gonna be an awful sorry person when ya got ta die alone," Chet thought to himself, as he moved away from the stranger and found another slot. Staring at the back of the head of the one he had tried to befriend, Chet wondered how a person could really believe such trash? Everyone needs friends. Still smarting from the rebuke he had received earlier; Chet stood silently looking neither to his left or right. Staring at the ground he was startled when a wad of tobacco juice barely missed the toe of his new boots.

"'bout got ya," the man standing to Chet's left said. "Sorry 'bout that. My aim's usually better 'en that." Chet looked into the grizzled face of a man at least twice his own age. The shaggy beard, deep-set eyes and bushy eyebrows gave him an almost primitive appearance. "My name's Nate Caldwell," the man said as he extended his hand to Chet. "From the looks 'a your duds ya ain't been in this here army no longer than I have. Still see the creases where they was folded in the box. Y'all from these parts, are ya?"

Despite the fellow's rugged appearance, he felt at ease with this giant of a man. Standing a good head and shoulders over Chet, the broad shoulders strained at the seams of the buttoned coat. Unlike Chet's trousers, which were turned up to form a cuff at the bottom, this man's pants were a good three inches above the ankles.

"Name's Baxter, Chet Baxter 'n I am from these parts. Pa's a blacksmith here in Hannibal 'n we got a farm out ta town a short ways." Pumping the offered hand Chet smiled. "I only joined up yesterday. Never thought I'd be leavin' home so soon. Why shucks, I ain't even got a rifle or nothin' yet. Y'all just joined up too?"

"Yea, I came up from Texas with a cattle drive ta Kansas. Had 'nuff 'a them dumb cows, so once I got paid I decided ta check out the country 'round here. Spent a few nights 'a playin' cards 'n drinkin' 'n I was broke again. When I heard they's needin' men ta help out, I figured this was as good a place as most ta join up. Fought in the tail end of the war with the Mex.'s 'n figured one war's pretty much like another, so here I am. At first they didn't want no old men like me, but when they found out I had fightin' experience they swore me right in." Another stream of tobacco juice hit the ground, causing Chet to move his feet closer together.

"Lookin' at this crowd, it don't look like most 'a them ever been in a schoolyard fight, much less a shootin' one. Some 'a them twerps they got runnin' 'round as officers ought ta still be home bouncin' on their Ma's knee."

"Attenn-tion," came the order from the front of the group. "There will be no more talking in the ranks. We will march in an orderly fashion to the train station now. There we will board a train and then, and only then, will you be told of our destination. There may be Federal spies among those assembled here, so it is imperative that our destination be kept secret. Right face, forward march."

The group of inexperienced soldiers strode, rather than marched, out of the square. The sight was almost comical as they either stepped on the heels of the man in front of them, or skipped to get into the rhythm of the cadence. Looking over his shoulder, Chet tried to find his folks and Cynthia in the crowd behind him, but to no avail.

The train yard was only a short three blocks from the square. The engine blew a cloud of steam from the side, as billows of black smoke poured from the stack. A string of open cars were connected to the boxcars, the latter would hold the horses and supplies.

Heavy cannons were tied down on three of the flatcars and on each corner of the platform an armed guard sat just above the wheels. More armed men sat atop each boxcar, while one accompanied the engineer and fireman in the cab of the engine. The regiment was halted alongside the tracks and then divided into three groups of thirty men each. Chet was more than pleased when the officer assigned to his group happened to be Keith Staten.

Once they had all found seats on the train's open cars the brakeman signaled to the engine and the train lurched forward. Gathering steam it slowly gained speed and before long they were leaving the outskirts of Hannibal, Missouri behind. The night air, combined with the moving train, sent a chill through Chet and he pulled the coat collar up around his face. In the darkness he made out the silhouettes of the trees as they sped past, and an occasional glimpse of the moon as it peeked from behind a cloud. He wasn't two hours out of town and already he was homesick. Reaching into his pocket he pulled out the necklace that Cynthia had placed there a short time ago. Fingering the heart-shaped fob he was thankful that the darkness hid the tears that were forming in his eyes. Clearing his throat, in an attempt to remove the lump that was near to being a sob, he tried to think of other things. Try as he may, his thoughts returned to those loved ones that would soon be sitting around the table at home. He wondered if perhaps Cynthia was laying across her bed crying for him?

"What do ya reckon's goin' on up there?" Nate Caldwell's voice brought him out of his reverie. The train began to slow as it approached a large fire and men with torches standing along side the tracks. "Can't be no robbers 'cause nobody'd be stupid 'nuff ta hold up a train loaded with soldiers," Nate said scratching his head.

As the train rolled to a halt, Keith Staten stood up. "Okay men, this is what you've been waiting to find out since we left Hannibal.

Jump down and form ranks in front of the car. Keep the noise down so the Colonel don't have ta yell, 'n he'll tell us what's goin' on." The light of the fire silhouetted the Confederate Colonel, the flickering of the flames reflected off the sword scabbard at his side as he stepped forward.

"Gentlemen," he shouted to be heard above the hiss of the engine, "as you may or may not know, the Union has vowed to hold any territory it has inside the Confederacy, by force if necessary.

There is a Yankee fort on an island out of the harbor of Charleston, South Carolina. Up to now it has been unmanned, but the Union forces have moved to put troops inside it. Because South Carolina led us in seceding and that island belongs to the State of South

Carolina, we are moving to take back what is rightfully ours. The Union is just as determined to hold the place they call Fort Sumter. The Confederacy is pulling troops from all over the south to reinforce the brigades there already. Gentlemen, I am afraid the war is about to began. This is not a conflict of 'Good verses Evil,' nor is it necessarily a matter of right or wrong. The long quarrel between the North and South over the interpretation of the U.S.

Constitution has let it come to this. We Southerners want the undefined powers to go to the individual States, while the Union wants the federal government to have all those powers. There are many on both sides of the line that disagree with the war and they may also be right. It is a matter of individual conscience and any of you that feel you can't condone this matter, are free to leave now.

I must tell you that Missouri has declared that it will join the ranks of the northern states should war be declared."

The colonel paused for any response and when no one stepped forward he continued speaking. "Because our regiment is made up of mostly untrained men, we will not be sent to the front immediately. Instead, we will be held in reserve and also act as a rear guard in case of a Union attack on our flank. Our current destination is Atlanta, Georgia. From there we will be dispersed to where ever we are needed the most. We shall pick up more troops along the way. The Confederate army has cut all train traffic from the north at the Virginia border. This will cut supply lines to the northern sympathizers living in the south. Some of them are helping runaway slaves to escape to the free north. The Southern Railway will still make the run south from Virginia. There will be more information later, but for now we need to be on our way again."

The men were loaded back onto the train, as the colonel walked to the only sleeping car on the tracks and mounted the steps. A wave of the lantern from the brakeman and the train jerked forward once more.

"Missouri joinin' the Union," Chet said softly. "Reckon that Ma was right 'bout this war gonna split families. He also remembered what Pa had said about Cynthia's father being an abolitionist. He sure hadn't acted like one, when he said they had big plans for him and their daughter. "Maybe he's one 'a them Copperheads."

"What say?" Nate asked. "You mumbled so low I couldn't hear the question. Somethin' 'bout Missouri, I think."

"Do ya reckon this war'll split families 'n friends 'fore it's over, Nate? I can't believe that a state that come inta the Union as a slave state, would join up with the Union when the chips were down. I know Bloody Kansas had their troubles, but I never figured Missouri ta back out."

"Sonny, it ain't gonna take no time for the split 'tween families, in fact it's already happened. Don't be too hard on Missouri. My state 'a Texas is a slave state only 'cause the politicians says so.

They let us inta the United States only if we'd enter as a slave state, ta pacify the lunk-heads dividin' the states. Yes sir, I got'ta feelin in my bones. This is gonna more than split families, it's gonna have one brother a killin' another, 'fore it's over."

CHAPTER FOUR.

"What do you mean we have to get off here? We have only been on this train for less than three days," An indignant Ida Kramer shouted into the face of the conductor. "We have paid for round trip tickets from Martindale, Pennsylvania to Rome, Georgia and that is precisely where we expect to go. This is a far cry from our destination and if necessary you had better move heaven and earth to get us there."

"Look lady. It wasn't us that closed the tracks; it was the Johnny Rebs that did that. If you have an argument with someone, take it up with Jeff Davis and his boys. All I know is, this train is turning around and heading back to Philadelphia, with or without you on board. Now, do you want to get off here and catch the Reb's train on to Rome or not? You'd best make up your mind soon, seeing as how we leave this station in ten minutes." The red faced man turned and walked away, leaving Ida standing in the isle-way fuming.

"Do we at least get the courtesy of having someone carry our bags for us?" She shouted after the conductor. The only response she received was a shake of his head as he disappeared through the doorway. "Somebody's certainly going to hear about this when we get back home. I have never received such shoddy treatment in my entire life. Come Connie, perhaps we can find a gentleman in this two-bit town that will help us. I have no idea where in the blue blazes we even are. One thing certain, I surely don't want to come here again."

"Don't get your dander up Aunt Ida. There is not a thing that we can do to alter what's happening, so I'd suggest that we just make the best of a bad situation. Who knows? It may even work to our advantage. Perhaps on the next train, we will be able to have a drawing room where we can even stretch our legs without hitting the opposite wall." Before they left the car Connie tried everything to pacify Ida and calm the older woman. "We carried our own bags to the depot back home and I'm certain we can manage again. It may even work out some of the kinks we accumulated on the ride from Pennsylvania."

As the April morning sun rose over the town Connie and Ida joined the rest of the disgruntled passengers on the platform. A line of people, just as irate as Ida Kramer had been, already formed at the window to the ticket office. The white-haired man inside was doing his best to explain the reason for the delay, but to no avail. A group of nine or ten Union soldiers milled about in an attempt to keep a riot from starting. When one angry passenger threw a rock through the depot window he was quickly escorted away by two burley soldiers.

"Ladies and gentlemen, could I have your attention please?" The voice came from a fairly young Union officer that was standing on one of the baggage carts. "I realize that you are being inconvenienced by this delay and I apologize. However there is nothing we can do about the situation. The Confederacy has declared themselves a Sovereign Nation, and as such they regulate everything within their borders. Unfortunately for us, that also means transportation. They now control everything south of the borders of Maryland and Virginia. There are on going discussions between both sides in an attempt to bring the States under one flag again, but this will take some time. Those of you that still wish to continue your journey south may carry your own luggage through that gate.

You will then be on the threshold of the Confederate States and be required to purchase another ticket to your destination. Once again, that is something we have no control over as the Southern Railway System regulates it. Just how long that train will make the run to Georgia, is anyone's guess. The Reb army has taken all except that one to haul troops. Those of you that wish to return to your point's to the north may do so by getting back on the same train you just left. Thank you for understanding our situation." With that he jumped to the ground and turned his back to the crowd.

"Well," Ida grumbled, "that's a fine kettle of fish. What are we to do now my dear? Turn around after coming all this way, or proceed on to Georgia?"

Ignoring the questions Connie hurried to the side of the man who had just spoken to them. Laying a hand on his arm, to halt his retreat, she said in the most polite tone she could muster. "I beg your pardon sir. Before we decide what we should do, would you be so kind as to answer a few questions for us?"

"I have noth.." the officer started to say as he attempted to pull his arm away from her touch. Turning his head he looked into her face. "Lady," he thought to himself, "I'd answer a thousand questions for that pretty face." He studied her from head to toe and the careful scrutiny made Connie blush, partly from embarrassment and partly from indignation at his forwardness. "Yes ma'am, I'd be happy to answer any questions that I can," he replied as he doffed his broad-brimmed hat.

"We are going to Rome, Georgia. However, before we proceed farther we need to know if there are any dangers associated with continuing on. My aunt and I are traveling alone and we don't wish to have any difficulties returning home. Our business should be completed in a week, possibly two at the most."

"As I mentioned before, the talks are going on continually between the two sides in this disagreement. I am certain that things will be worked out shortly and everything will return to normal. The Confederacy is only making a lot of noise is all. I highly doubt that they would do anything silly. The Union has three times the men; we are better equipped and have more resources than the Rebs do. It would be downright folly for them to start something. No ma'am, I doubt that you and your aunt will have any real problems returning home."

"I thank you sir, for your kindness. You have made us feel much better about the situation. Come Aunt Ida, the Major has answered most of our questions." Connie picked up her bags and turned to walk away.

"It's Captain ma'am, and if I may be so bold I would like to buy you and your aunt a cup of tea before you leave." His eyes continued to travel from her face to her figure. "Just my luck," he thought to himself, "I finally meet a woman with a face of a Goddess and she has to have an old aunt for a chaperone."

"Young man," Ida snapped at him, "it's not a cup of tea you're interested in, nor is it her aunt. If you'll be so kind as to put your eyes back in your head we'll move on. Come Dear, we mustn't miss our train." Taking Connie by the arm she guided the girl around the officer and toward the gate. "Young whipper-snapper must think all women are either stupid or blind to his blarney. A cup of tea indeed, I know what he had in mind and it wasn't studying tea leaves in the bottom of a cup either."

Connie chuckled at Ida's indignation. "I thought he was rather handsome," she goaded the older woman, "one could certainly do worse than to marry a Union officer."

"It wasn't marriage he had in mind either. Constance Garner, I'm surprised at you. Are you really so naïve as to believe that man was only interested in conversation? You and I need to have a long talk about men." The shocked look on Ida's face made Connie burst out laughing.

"My dear Aunt Ida, I am neither stupid nor am I blind. That soldier wasn't the first to make a pass at me. Mother had that talk with me years ago and what she left out, I have managed to learn myself. I'm sorry for teasing you, but the look on your face was priceless. I promise to try to behave in a more lady-like manner in the future."

Just beyond the gate stood a makeshift ticket office. The man inside was just as besieged with irate people as the poor fellow on the other side of the barrier. Scribbled on a painted board in chalk were the arrival and departure times for trains, along with prices to various destinations. When the two women reached the window Ida once again vented her anger upon the poor soul inside.

"What do you mean we have to buy another ticket? We pur-chased tickets to Rome, Georgia and by crackey that's where we want to go. I want to speak to whoever is in charge of this mess, and I want to do it right now." Connie was thankful for the bars on the small window that separated the man from the outside. She was certain that Ida would have dragged the fellow through the opening if they weren't there.

"Look Lady, it won't do ya no good ta talk ta nobody. Them's the rules. Ya either buy a ticket or you don't get on the train, it's simple as that. Now, do ya want a ticket or don't ya? If not move aside so I can take care 'a the people behind ya. We got a schedule ta meet 'n I don't need no more hassle from y'all. Two tickets ta Rome, Georgia comes ta thirty-five dollars Confederate or forty dollars Union, do ya want 'em or not?"

The way the veins in her head stood out Connie was afraid that Ida would have an attack of apoplexy. Her anger was out of control at this unexpected treatment. Through clenched teeth she muttered, "You little no account pip-squeak. For two cents I'd come through this window and teach you the proper way to talk to a lady."

Knowing that he was completely safe behind the barred window, and having had quite enough abuse, the man just smiled as he replied. "I already know how to talk ta a lady, 'n when I see one I'll be proper. Now make up your mind 'bout what you're gonna do grandma, go or stay."

Before Ida would lose complete control of herself, Connie pulled her aside and stood before the window. "Two tickets to Rome please and we'd like a compartment." Opening her purse she counted out forty dollars and passed it under the narrow opening between the bars and counter. "Would you be so kind as to tell me when the next train leaves, that will take us on to Georgia?"

"Sure can ma'am," the ticket agent smiled at her as he checked the old clock behind him,

"It'll be leavin' in forty-five minutes. That 'un said nothin' 'bout no compartment, that's 'nother six dollars Union." Connie paid the difference and the fellow pushed the tickets through the slot under the bars. Leaning forward he half-whispered, "If that ol' bat's with y'all, I suggest ya keep her on a short leash 'n muzzled. Folks down here 'bout had 'nuff 'a that Yankee pushin' 'round 'n don't take kindly ta bein' bullied."

Turning on her heels she pulled Ida away before she could continue the tirade. Ushering her to a seat on the platform, she forced the older woman to sit down. Ida was so furious that her hands were shaking, as she folded them in her lap. Sitting beside her Connie wrapped both arms around Ida and pulled her close.

"Don't let this matter upset you so. We'll be at Cyprus Wood in a day or two and you'll have all the house servants to fuss over you. I remember how they filled my bath water and put handfuls of jasmine petals in it to make me smell sweet. It's strange what things an eight-year-old mind tucks away. Grandpa and Grandma Garner took us on a picnic and I met Moses. He was one of grandpa's slaves, but he was more of an overseer. I wonder if he is still there? He was big and the blackest man I had ever seen in my life, yet also the most gentle. He used to give me piggyback rides around the front yard."

"I'm far too old for someone to be giving me a bath," Ida sighed. "I do like the idea of the jasmine though. Bye the way. In case it has slipped your mind, you're a bit too old to be carried piggyback now. Of course that shave tail soldier on the platform wouldn't have minded carrying you around."

"Y'all want ta buy a paper, ladies?" Connie shifted her gaze from Ida to the boy before them. A lad of about ten held a stack of newspapers in one arm and one folded in half in his other hand. "Newspaper? Latest on all the goin's on here 'bouts." The freckled face appeared not to have seen soap and water since last year. The coveralls were patches held together by threads and Connie noticed he was also barefoot.

"Sure, I'll take a newspaper," she said, smiling at the youngster. "How much is it?"

"Five cents Confederate 'n ten cents Union," the boy replied as he held the folded paper out to Connie. "All the latest news too," he grinned.

Reaching into her purse, she took out fifty cents and pressed it into the boy's hand. "Ten cents for the paper and forty cents for you being so good looking."

"Gee thanks, lady," the lad beamed, "thanks a lot. Been a long time since I made four-bits in one day." Pocketing the coin he turned away, only to be called back by Ida who had opened the paper.

"This paper is dated April second, eighteen hundred and sixty one. Any fool knows that today is April the fourth. What are trying to pull by selling us a two-day-old newspaper? Do you take us for idiots?" The stern look on the woman's wrinkled face half-frightened and half amused the youngster.

"Seein' as how I don't know ya ma'am, I really can't say if you're an idiot or not. This paper only comes out one time 'a week, 'n what's news then's, still news now." Tipping his straw hat, he moved off to hawk more of his newspapers. Speechless at the boy's audacity Ida sat with her mouth agape, as the lad turned and gave her a sly wink before disappearing into the crowd. Connie bowed her head so the wide brim of her hat would hide the smile that she couldn't stop from spreading.

"I'm certainly flattered by all of this Southern hospitality," Ida exploded once more. "Rather than fight for this sorry pile of dirt, we'd be better off setting fire to all of it and bury the ashes." The train whistle drowned out the rest of her anger as the Southern Railway engine preceded the rest of the cars into the station. Rolling to a stop directly before the two women it expelled a cloud of steam. Once again Ida was certain that the insult was aimed at her personally.

The compartment was a mirror image of the one they had on the train when they left home. Pulling the blind closed Ida slumped into one of the chairs. "I have never been a drinking woman but I'm about ready to give it a try. There must be something to it, because my poor dead husband certainly tried it enough. I think we'd better eat something out of this basket. I swear my right arm's two foot longer from hauling it around." Opening the picnic basket she began to spread the assortment of goodies on the table before her.

"Perhaps we..." That was as far as Connie got with her warning. A long blast of the whistle and the engine jerked the train into motion, dumping the majority of the food into Ida's lap and the remainder on the floor. "I was going to say, 'Perhaps we should wait until the train is underway before we unpack the basket.'" Picking the food from her skirt Ida shook her head in disbelief.

"My father used to say a poem to me when I was little and things like this happened. It was called, 'Why Me?' I don't remember at all, but the first lines went something like this."

"Have you ever had a day, my friend, when nothing would go right?

When everything possible will go wrong, though you try with all your might."

"Well, I'm having one of those days. Perhaps we can get all the aggravating things over in one day and enjoy the rest of the trip. At least I saved most of the food from hitting the floor."

"You aren't wearing the bottle of pickles either," Connie added as she held the basket tightly. The companions looked at one another and burst out laughing. "One thing about traveling with you Aunt Ida, it's never dull." Helping the older woman pick the food from her dress, Connie thought of the many times Ida had cleaned up the messes that she had made as a youngster. "Don't waste what others would gladly eat," she said, brushing off the loaf of bread and carefully placing it back on the table. "That's what you always told me anyway."

During the days that followed the train meandered on, through the rolling hills of Virginia, across the narrow neck of North Carolina, near Asheville and entered Georgia. At every station, and all along the way, they saw groups of soldiers wearing the Confederate gray pushing north. Horses pulling large cannons and wagons loaded with armed troops lined the roads. In the cramped compartment the three days on this train seemed like three months. Ida and Connie made it a practice of stepping outside of the small room and taking a few daily walks up and down the aisle. It was on one of these strolls that they noticed a particularly large gathering of soldiers, standing at the station, as they entered Gainesville, Georgia.

The train slowed then ground to a halt before the platform. The women watched from the train window then nonchalantly continued their constitutional down the aisle. The locomotive had no more than came to a complete stop, when the doors at either end of the car opened and soldiers carrying bayoneted rifles blocked the exits.

"If you ladies'd be so kind as to return to your seats, please?" The man behind them stated politely. "I'm deeply sorry for the inconvenience. This'll only take a moment and y'all can be on your way again." As Ida and Connie entered their compartment the young man stood in the doorway. "Leave the door open, if y'all don't mind."

"May I ask what this is all about?" Connie asked, in the most polite tone that she could use under the circumstances. "I assure you sir, that we have done nothing wrong. We are simply traveling to my late grandfather's plantation near Rome. The many delays, we have encountered so far, cause me to wonder if we may not make it by next Christmas."

The soldier smiled. "Y'all shouldn't have no problem makin' Rome by Christmas. That's over eight months away 'n Rome's less than a hundred 'n ten miles. Once the train gets goin' again, y'all ought ta be in Rome in a day or so. There's gonna be a couple 'a detours ta take on some more troops, so that's gonna delay ya a bit."

"Is there a problem here private?" A deep voice demanded. The one asking the question was out of the line of vision of the two women inside the car. Connie could only catch a glimpse of the brim of a gray hat.

The private turned in the direction of the voice and snapped to attention. "No sir. There ain't no problem, no problem at all. I was just talkin' ta these ladies while I was waitin' for y'all ta come 'n question 'em."

"You make it sound like an inquisition, Private." A tall and very handsome man, wearing the insignia of Major on his Confederate uniform, stepped around the doorway and into the compartment. "If you ladies will excuse this intrusion, you will not be delayed very long. The unpleasant task of searching every train from inside out, has fallen on the shoulders of my men and myself." Removing his hat, he let his eyes scan from Connie to Ida and back again. "May I ask where you are coming from and what your final destination is to be?"

"We came from Philadelphia and we hope to reach Rome, Georgia sometime this year. With all these interruptions, I have my doubts of ever reaching there." Connie was normally not so flippant, however her patience was wearing very thin.

Ignoring her sarcasm the officer smiled. "May I see your tickets please? I also need you ladies to step out into the aisle." Connie produced the four tickets and handed them to the Major, who scanned them carefully. "According to the Southern Railway tickets, you are indeed going to Rome. However, the tickets on the Union railway show that you left Martindale, not Philadelphia, as you told me. Could you please explain the discrepancy?"

"That's really very simple," Connie replied, as she and Ida were ushered out of the compartment. "Nobody has ever heard of

Martindale, while everyone knows of Philadelphia. They are but a few miles apart, and it saves a lot of explaining about where we are from by saying we live in Philadelphia. If that is a capital crime in the South, then I suppose we are guilty. If not, I would appreciate an explanation as to why those men are going through our luggage? There are personal items that I hardly want men gawking at."

"It isn't a crime of any kind ma'am. We have orders to search for anything suspicious, or contraband of any kind. Your effects will be restored to their proper place, but we can hardly search baggage without disturbing things, no matter how private they may be. As for no one ever hearing of your hometown, I am very familiar with Martindale. One of my classmates at the Academy was from Philadelphia, and we spent time touring around there on weekends and holidays. He used to show me the quaint houses along the main street there. He was justly proud of the history associated with that area."

"Sir. I think we got a problem in here," a soldier called from inside the compartment. Both women craned their necks to look past the officer as he walked past them and into the room. The young man, who had first met them at the door, was going through the picnic basket. Inside the folds he pulled out the derringer pistol and held it at arms length.

"Would you ladies care to explain exactly what you plan to do with this?" His eyes had changed from soft and sympathetic, to hard and accusing.

"That belongs to me," snapped Ida. "If you think two women would travel alone into unknown country without some kind of protection, you're crazy as a loon. My late husband gave me that, and from what I've seen of the South we may need it before we can get back home. If you'll put it back where it was, it would be appreciated."

Returning the pistol to the basket his face once again softened. "I don't see any real harm you could do with that little thing. Please, just don't shoot anyone with it. I hate the paperwork associated with those kind of things."

"Exactly where are you from, anyway?" Ida asked. "You certainly don't talk like a Johnny Reb, more like a real person," her ire raised at the infernal delays.

"I'm originally from Roanoke, Virginia. However I was sent to Child's Military School, in Providence, Rhode Island, where I was schooled until I was able to enter the Academy. As for the, 'Johnny Reb,' part. That is a nickname that the Union has given us. We are not Rebels in the slightest. We are only asking for an equal voice in Congress and rights that have been ours since this nation was founded. Our stand was not a matter of choice, but one of necessity.'"

"That is the second time that you have referred to the, 'Academy,'" Connie said. "Exactly what Academy are you referring to?"

"Why, West Point Academy of course. I graduated from there nearly five years ago, and very proud of the fact. My father was a military man, as was my grandfather. Grandpa fought with George Washington."

"Somehow I never figured a Reb to go to West Point, much less graduate," Ida dug the insults deeper.

Ignoring the sarcasm, the young officer smiled. "It may interest you to know, that our General Robert E. Lee was also a graduate of West Point. In fact, he not only graduated, he did so ranking second in his class. We have quite a number of graduates in our ranks."

"I reckon that 'bout does it Major. Ain't found nothin' in there, 'ceptin' that there pistol." The two soldiers filed past and into the aisle way.

"I thank you for your patience and again I apologize for the delay. You ladies may return to your room now." Replacing the hat on his head he turned to go.

"You never did tell us exactly what it is you were looking for," Connie attempted to make amends for Ida's rudeness.

"There have been a number of northern spies that have infiltrated the south. There could be considerable harm done if they were allowed to pass information to their confederates up north. It is our job to filter out these people and arrest them. Goodbye ladies, and do have the rest of an enjoyable journey."

It was not long after that, when the whistle sounded and the train resumed it's rattling down the tracks. Connie and Ida sat in silence, each absorbed in their own thoughts. They were in the same positions when the porter came to pull down their bunks for the night. Climbing into their respective beds they were soon put to sleep by the swaying of the train, much like a baby would be in a rocking chair.

Slivers of daylight touched Connie on the face as the locomotive pulled it's load around curves and on to straight-aways. The narrow bed made turning over nearly impossible, without rolling onto the floor. Raising herself onto one elbow she attempted to bounce her body onto the other side.

"Are you awake, Connie?" Ida's voice was barely above a whisper.

"I'm sorry if I woke you. I'm trying to turn over and one must be a contortionist to manage that trick. I know the person that built these beds was the same one that devised the medieval devices of torture." Connie finally gave up the fight and sat on the edge of the bed.

"You didn't wake me. I've been laying here thinking about something that officer said. Why do you suppose the Confederacy is so concerned about the Union finding out about their troop movement? As far as I can figure, there's only one reason for such deep dark secrecy. I think we are closer to an all out shooting war than we realize." The concern in Ida's voice bothered Connie. Never before had she heard this tone. Usually Ida was the take-charge person who would twist the tail of Satan himself, if he got in her way. "Have you noticed that all the troops are moving north? I haven't seen one column going any other direction. Why would the south be so concerned about northern spies that they would search every train coming from the north? Too many things make two plus two equal six, as far as I'm concerned."

Before answering Ida's questions Connie pondered on the things she had mentioned. It was true that the troop movements had all appeared to be moving north, and the spy question had bothered her also. The prospect of all out war had never crossed her mind, and even-now she attempted to push it from her thoughts. There must be a simpler answer, however the more she thought about it, the more sense Ida was making.

"Perhaps we should send a message to Mister Judd at Cyprus Wood telling him to sell the plantation. We could catch the next train north and get out of here, just in case you are right. I wish I had listened to my premonitions and stayed at home. I'm dreadfully sorry for involving you in this, dear Ida. You are so much older and wiser than I, what do you think we should do?"

"I appreciate the, 'Wiser,' part, but you could well have left out the, 'So much older,' bit,'" Ida laughed. "Honey, I am just as much in the dark as you are. We would feel like fools if we turned for home and nothing happened, but even bigger fools if we get caught between two sides shooting at each other. At my age the only thing that my intuition tells me is when it's time to eat, sleep and go to the bathroom. Perhaps we should pray for the solution. That Man up there has seen me through some pretty harrowing scrapes and never let me down yet." Together the two companions knelt by the side of the table and each prayed silently. They had just finished when the train slowed as it entered the station.

The train depot at Rome was a mixture of old Southern charm and big city confusion. Piles of cotton-bales bound for England and France crowded the platform, while lines of Blacks unloaded more from the string of wagons along side of the station. Gray uniforms were scattered here and there, but not in the concentration that they had been seen previously. As they stepped from the train onto the platform both women lowered their heads against the bright sun.

"Is that you, Miss Constance?" A male voice called from the edge of the station. "It is y'all. Ol' Moses'd know them pretty curls anywheres. My, my, how you growed. Last time I saw y'all, ya was no bigger 'en Ceil's churn." Moses hurried toward her as fast as his aged body allowed. Bowing to the women he politely took the luggage from their hands. "It sure is grand ta see y'all again. Ceil, she been up all night bakin' them little cakes ya liked so much for breakfast. She been nearly workin' me ta death scaldin' a hog for ta make your pork chops out 'a. She ain't forgot how much y'all likes 'em for your supper. No sah, there ain't a whole bunch she don't remember 'bout little ol' Constance. We best hurry 'long 'fore she thinks I been dallyin' 'n gives me, 'What for,' when we get home. Masta Tom, he would 'a come for y'all himself, 'ceptin that he got some important business he got ta take care 'a at Cyprus Wood. Sends his apologies though, he does.'"

"How is dear Ceil?" Connie asked Moses about his wife. "I

will always remember how she was always trying to get more food down me. She kept telling me that it wasn't healthy to be as tiny as I was, and how she was going to put some meat on my bones. I'm afraid that if I had eaten all she wanted me to, I would have been as big around as her churn also."

"Ol' Ceil, she jus' fine. She's 'bout like Moses, getting' ol' 'n worn out 'n puttin' on more 'roun' the middle 'n slowin' down some. She still cooks up the finest vittles in the whole 'a Georgia though. Starts early 'n stays up 'til the rest are in bed. I swear that woman's like a mother hen with a whole yard 'a chicks ta tend. Can't complain though, 'cause she sure takes good care 'a her man, she does."

"Moses, I'd like you to meet my Aunt Ida. She was kind enough to accompany me on this long journey. I would have been lost without her. Aunt Ida, this is the most incredible man on all of Cyprus Wood Plantation. He is the one I told you about, who would give me piggy-back rides around the front yard."

"I'm very pleased ta meet ya, ma'am." Unable to bow because he had both arms full of luggage, Moses simply displayed a mouthful of white teeth in a wide grin and nodded. "I don't reckon I 'member Master Ham or Mistress Anna sayin' nothin' 'bout no child named Ida."

"I'm very pleased to make your acquaintance also, Mister Moses. Connie has told me so much about you, that I almost knew you before we met. I'm not really Connie's aunt, we are simply good friends. I have watched her grow into a young woman and am closer to her than if we were blood relatives." Turning to Connie she added, "My goodness, he is a big man. No wonder he could carry you around on his back all day. I don't believe that I have ever seen such a perfect specimen of manhood, even at his age"

Moses beamed at the thought that he had been the topic of conversation among these white women. Arriving at the carriage he placed the luggage into the carrier on the back, and then hurried to help the ladies into their seats. It was with a bit of difficulty that he pulled himself into the seat and with a slap of the reins, the final leg of the journey began.

"Moses, were you there when Grandfather passed away? He was such a kind and gentleperson, that at times I found it hard to believe that he was actually a slave owner. The picture Aunt Phoebe painted was of cruel men wielding whips over the backs of starved black people. I saw nothing of that when I was there. Tell me Moses, and I want the truth. Was it all an act for my benefit, or were the slaves really treated the way I saw them treated?"

"Mistress Constance, in all the time I been at Cyprus Wood I never seen even one whippin'. I seen your grandpappy crack a head or two in his day, but them folks had it a comin' ta 'em." Turning in the seat to face Connie, the huge Negro's eyes almost were pleading for her to believe him. "I know some places 'round the south don't treat us folks proper. Your grandpa got inta more 'n one shovin' match with folks what tol' him he was breedin' a rebellion, 'cause he was teachin' black folk ta read. Seems some white folk are afraid that if a man like me gets too smart, he's gonna start thinkin' on his own 'n cause trouble. Master Ham, he teaches me ta read some 'n he treated me like a man, not a ol' shoe to throw ta the dogs. He ain't never held much stock in havin' ignorant house servants 'round him." Facing towards the front again, Connie saw the broad shoulders slump. "Yes Miss Constance, I was there when Master Ham done passed on. Only one day in my whole life that was any sadder than that one." The voice grew softer, then silence followed. Not wishing to push the subject, Connie let it lay.

Even though it was only the early days of April, the humidity was stifling. Perspiration soaked the shirt of the man in the driver's seat and the women fanned themselves with their handkerchiefs. Connie remembered the fan, which always hung on the wrist of her grandmother, and now knew that it was far more than an ornament. Just as they thought the trip would never end the carriage turned into the tree-lined lane. Ahead was the white mansion that Connie remembered playing in as a child. It was just as she remembered, except the magnolia bushes had grown to miniature trees and grandmother's rose garden no longer graced the front.

"We's here," Moses announced as he pulled the team to a halt. "Hope y'all's hungry, 'cause I know fer a fact that Ceil's got 'nuff vittles ta feed the whole Confederate army waitin' for ya." He had no more than climbed down from the seat when the front door of the house opened and a plump woman bounced down the stairs.

"Missie Constance, we's sure glad ta see ya back at Cyprus

Wood." The red bandana covering her head showed tight curls of white hair peeking from beneath it. The broad grin displayed yellowing teeth that had an exceptionally wide gap between the two in front. Pushing Moses aside she helped Connie and Ida from the carriage. "Ya shiftless good for nothin'," she said turning to Moses. "Move them ol' bones 'n fetch the luggage. These ladies probably starvin' ta death 'n you're takin your time gettin' here. Where ya been anyhow?"

Throwing up his arms in frustration, Moses glared at his wife. "Can't very well fetch 'em here 'fore the train comes in, now can I? I was waitin' right at the platform when they come in 'n loaded the stuff 'n came right here. Didn't do no dallyin' neither." He glanced at Connie, as if for conformation that what he had said was true.

"What Moses said is true," Connie quickly agreed with his story. " There were so many delays that we were beginning to wonder if we would ever arrive." With Ceil leading the way, the rest followed her into the foyer of the mansion. This was also as Connie remembered it. The prisms in the cut glass windows cast rainbows of color wherever the sunlight landed. The stairway, leading to the upstairs bedrooms, was still polished to a high sheen, as was the mahogany table just inside the entryway. The crystal chandelier was just as she remembered, with it's hanging bobbles reflecting the sunlight. Ceil ushered them into the sitting room and brushed imaginary dust from the settee before indicating for them to have a seat.

"Masta Tom, he ain't here yet. He had business he had ta take care of in town. Sends his apologies for not bein' here ta meet y'all though." Ceil busied herself fluffing the pillows on the arms of the settee then turned to Moses, who was standing in the arched doorway.

"Take Miss Constance' bag ta the master bedroom 'n the other lady's ta the one 'cross the hall. Make sure they's clean water in the basin 'n pitcher too. We didn't know y'all was bringin' company with ya or we'd have had everythin' ready," Ceil apologized, glancing at Ida.

"What we'd appreciate more than anything right now, is a nice bath," Connie said, after she had introduced Ida to Ceil. "It seems forever since I have been able to soak in a nice tub. Do you still put those jasmine petals in the water? I remember that as much as anything else at Cyprus Wood."

"I'll tend ta that bath soon as I can. Got ta heat more water first, 'n y'all can be eatin' while it's gettin' done. I'll get Savannah ta take ya to your rooms so's ya can clean up while I'm settin' out the food." Ceil left the women alone, only to reappear shortly with a young girl in tow. Connie guessed that she was approximately the same age as herself, give or take a year or two either way, and strikingly pretty. Her flawless olive complexion was a direct contrast to the extremely dark color of both Ceil and Moses. "This here's Savannah. She gonna be your servant long as you're here. T'ain't no house servant in all the south better 'en this one."

"I am very pleased to make your acquaintance," the girl spoke in flawless English, as she curtseyed. "If there is anything that I can do to make your stay more comfortable, please let me know." Connie and Ida looked at each other in amazement. There was not even the slightest hint of the drawl that most Southerners displayed. "Ceil has told me of your wishes and I shall have the tubs brought to the kitchen. Your baths will be ready as soon as you have finished eating. If you will follow me I shall take you to your rooms where you can wash." Stepping aside she waited for Connie and Ida to precede her from the room, then she led them upstairs and to their individual bedrooms.

"That girl intrigues me," Connie thought to herself. "I must learn more about her. I believe there is more to her than meets the eye, much more. The way she carries herself, the immaculate appearance, her impeccable speech, there is nothing about her that even hints of a house servant."

CHAPTER FIVE.

As more cars full of troops were added at every stop, the ancient steam engine was having a hard time pulling even the smallest hill. The line now extended well beyond the limits of the old boiler to produce enough steam to drive the wheels.

"I'm a wonderin' if the war'll be over by the time we get there," Nate Caldwell grumbled to Chet. "I been on milk runs 'fore, but nothin' as slow as this one. A body freezes to death at night 'n roasts durin' the day on these here open cars. Ya can bet that high falootin' colonel ain't hurtin' none in that there nice car he's ridin' in. At this rate we won't even see Georgia for another month or more. Once we hit the border we still got a ways ta go 'fore we get ta Atlanta."

"T'ain't as bad as all that," Chet attempted to relieve some of the hostilities that were continually growing inside of his traveling companion. "We get two square meals a day 'n a warm blanket ta throw over us at night. If it weren't for your blamed snorin' I'd be sleepin' like a baby. I ain't heard noise like that since Pa scalded the last hog. I bet your kin clear down in Texas hear that noise 'n say, 'That's ol' Nate. At it again.'" Jabbing an elbow into the ribs of the Texan, Chet hoped to get his mind on something besides their slow progress.

"What y'all mean, 'My snorin,?' Never snored in my whole life. I know, 'cause I ain't had no complaints from none 'a the gals I bedded. Y'all know how women are. If ya got a fault, they pick up on it right now, 'n they sure let a man know about it.'" The grin on Nate's face told Chet that he had accomplished what he wanted.

"I figure that when we get ta Atlanta, I'm goin' ta ask ta be transferred ta the front. They have ta need experienced fightin' men up there 'n I sure didn't sign up ta baby sit y'all. I'd rather take a Yankee bullet than have ta change y'all's diapers for the rest 'a the war. There ain't even a whisker one on yer face yet. Can't even see that there peach fuzz on your chin less the light hits it just right." The insults were no longer humorous to Chet. When they started attacking his manhood, he took it personal.

"I seen that bald spot a formin' on the back 'a your head," Chet retaliated. "Least ways I don't grow wild on my face what should grow natural on my head. Ya could hide a whole regiment inside that mess ya call a beard." Satisfied that he had evened the score he sat back in his seat and watched the scenery slowly pass by.

He sat in silence and his thoughts turned to home. The river would be just starting to warm up from the cool weather, and the fish would begin to feed. He imagined that his brothers would once again be cutting school and be sitting along the bank. He envisioned them sitting with their legs crossed and the cane poles draped over their knees, lost in conversation of the many important events in their young lives. Whether worms or liver was the best bait for catfish, or if they should hide another dead fish in Old Lady Hemmingway's desk drawer again? He smiled at the memory of doing just that the year before. The stench had become overwhelming before she discovered it, where he had tucked neatly in the folds of her papers at the bottom of her drawer. Immediately it was one of the Baxter boys that got blamed for the dastardly deed, but lack of evidence kept them from being punished. Remembering the hours spent behind the hand plow attempting to make furrows in the unyielding soil of home. He would even settle for the chore of plowing through the rocks, if he could only join the family in one more happy night together. His mind slipped from one memory to another, each more enjoyable than the last.

In actuality, Chet could not have been more wrong. The home was not the happy domicile that he had left behind. His hometown had become a place of suspicion and loathing. Since the telegraph key first clicked word of the attack on Fort Sumter nothing was the same there. Factions on both sides of the issue eyed the other with suspicion and downright hatred. The school had closed, as had Pa's blacksmith shop and many of the other places of business in town. People were fearful of leaving their homes and the opposition had burned out many. Groups of hooded horsemen plagued the countryside, driving out anyone who dared to oppose them. Pillars of smoke marked where proslavery families once lived, only to be followed by another where an abolitionist home was destroyed. Lorenzo and Samantha Baxter and their three boys sat around the kitchen table.

"Things have got completely out of control here in Missouri," a tired looking Lorenzo said to his family. "Things in Kansas are just as bad 'n it's just a matter 'a time 'fore we get hit. They already burned out the Harris family 'n I hear they shot Cynthia's pa. It was bad 'nuff when they was just burnin' folk's homes, but now they's started ta kill 'em too. Mrs. Harris loaded the rest 'a the family on a train ta somewhere. Don't know where they was goin', they just packed up what wasn't burned 'n left. Ma 'n me been doin' some talkin' 'n we think we best pack up 'n move. Y'all know how I feel 'bout this war, but seems like there ain't no more sittin' astraddle the fence. I see good 'n bad in both sides. I ain't sayin' that the South's all in the right, but I don't see where the Union's right in bein' able ta kill the livelihood of the South neither.

We all's goin' ta have a say in where we should go 'n then we vote on it. I done traded all the livestock 'n chickens ta a fella for a broken-down team 'a mules 'n a dilapidated wagon. With the horses 'n wagon we already got, we ought 'ta be able ta make it wherever we want." Usually, when Pa tamped tobacco into his pipe it meant the conversation was over. This time it was barely beginning.

"How's Chet gonna find us if we move?" A very disturbed Tim asked. Having never lived anyplace else, he was more than apprehensive about leaving the comfort of Hannibal. "I vote that if'n we got ta move, we go where Chet is."

"How we gonna do sometnin' like that, stupid?" Scoffed Chad at the suggestion made by his little brother. "We don't even know where they done sent Chet, 'n 'sides findin' him'd be near impossible. Might as well try ta find a blue-eyed catfish as findin' him in all them gray uniforms. I vote that we head for anywhere they don't let them Yankees boss ya 'round. Maybe Texas'd be a good spot. They joined the Confederacy 'n it ain't too far away neither."

"We have no way to let Chet know 'bout our plans, Tim," Ma said, in an attempt to put his young mind at ease. "Chad, ya got no call ta call your brother names 'n I don't want ta hear no more 'a it.

He got as much right ta his say as y'all do." A chastened Chad mumbled a curt apology to Tim before taking a sip from his coffee cup. "I vote we go to the place least likely for fightin' ta be," she continued. "I heard the Utah Territory's been sectioned off 'n a new state called, 'Nevada,' has been broke off it. The Union's pushin' strong for it ta be joinin' the north, but there ain't supposed ta be no fightin' there. I'm tired 'a war 'n even the talk 'a war. I want ta go where I don't got ta worry 'bout my boys gettin' shot.'" Tears welled up in the tired blue eyes as she finished speaking.

"I think we ought ta head for Virginia. Ol' La….," Tad stopped in mid-word, for he remembered the tongue-lashing Ma had given him once before for being disrespectful to an adult. All he had called her was, "Ol' Lady Hemmingway," 'n every kid in school did that. Ma had given him a heavy what-for and told him to watch his mouth in the future. "Miss Hemmingway come from Richmond, Virginia, 'n to hear her tell it, there ain't no better place on earth. It's got good huntin', 'n the fishin's supposed ta be great. Lots 'a land for us ta farm 'n everythin's green. That's my vote."

"It looks like everybody wants ta go in a different direction," Pa said, as he struck a fresh match to the pipe. "We ain't never gonna get nowhere this way. Seein' as how we can't stay here, we got ta settle on a place ta go. Tim, ya ain't had your say yet 'n it's got ta be somewheres other than Missouri."

"I reckon that if we got ta go, I vote with Tad. Heard 'bout them savages out west that take a person's hair 'n I'm kind'a partial ta keepin' mine." Glaring at Chad, for the remark about him being stupid, he continued. "Texas ain't no good, heard there ain't nothin' but sand 'n scorpions down there. Anybody that wants ta move there got ta have chicken manure for brains." Smiling at getting even for his brother's insult, Tim sat back in his chair. "I vote Virginia too."

The debate went on well into the night. Sometime during the discussion Tim fell asleep, his head resting on his folded arms. Chad finally withdrew his vote for Texas and joined the other two for Virginia, but Ma wouldn't budge from Nevada. Her husband saw good and bad in both selections. The west was a wild unknown quantity, while Virginia was close to the fighting. To move his family into the vast and inhospitable west was something that he would have to ponder for a time, and time was way too short. Deserters of the armies from both sides found easy pickings in both Kansas and Missouri. They had learned from the war that taking what they wanted by force was far easier than paying for it. Gangs from both factions roamed the territories, pillaging and burning as they went. There was no law left to control either these bandits or the hooded political vigilantes, which rode unimpeded and unchallenged through the territory.

"This is the way I figure it," Pa said solemnly. "We can be on our way out 'a Missouri in five days. I figure that'll give me time ta sell off what we don't want ta take with. Reckon that I can get a few dollars for the tools at the shop, ain't much call for 'em anyhow. Only shod one mule in the past two weeks. Seems nobody trusts nobody else now days." Taking his wife by the hand he looked at her, as she could never remember him ever doing before. "My Dear, I got ta vote with the boys. Nevada's still wild 'n that's what we're tryin' ta get away from here in Missouri. Maybe we can find us a spot in Virginia. Somewhere we can farm a plot away from everybody else 'n we won't be bothered. I'm sorry, but it looks like you're out voted. We start gettin' things together tomorrow 'n leave come nightfall," pausing to count on his fingers, "next Tuesday.

Nobody can know what we're planin'. We'll go on doin' what we do everyday, just like always. You boys'll go fishin', 'n Ma can do whatever it is she does around the house. We'll put the wagons in the barn 'n load 'em after dark. I'll pretend that 'cause business has slowed I'm sellin' the tools ta feed the family. Ma, I want ya ta be sure ta impress on Tim how important it is ta be quiet 'bout this.

I reckon we all best get ta bed now. It's gonna be a busy week ahead 'n we're gonna be stayin' up most nights gettin' ready." With that Pa awakened Tim and they all went to their respective beds, each thinking of the next few days and the uncertainty that faced them.

The short nap had refreshed Tim and he lay in the darkness, his hands folded behind his head. "How would Chet have voted, if he had been here? What if they moved and Chet never found them when he came home?" "What if's," came one after another until his mind was boggled with confusing thoughts. When he could no longer focus on one problem or another, he climbed from his bed and quietly walked to the window. Kneeling on the rough board floor he folded his hands and looked heavenward.

"Dear Lord, I need some help 'n I need it bad. It looks like we're gonna move 'n I'm worried 'bout Chet a findin' us when he gets home. Things don't look so good here in Missouri, 'n Pa's takin' us all out ta here. Please help us out as we travel 'n watch over Chet. Don't let nothin' bad happen ta him so he can be safe 'n come home okay. I know You're busy with the war 'n all, but I'd sure appreciate it if Y'all could see the way clear ta help us out." Tim paused to ponder if there was anything that he had left out before closing his prayer. "There is one other thing. If Ya got a mind ta, would Ya guide Pa ta a place where they's pretty good fishin' too? I reckon that's 'bout all I got ta say. Amen."

"What in the name of Ned are ya doin over there?" whispered Chad from his bed. The voice startled Tim, who immediately jumped to his feet.

"Ain't doin' nothin'," he replied quietly. "Just a lookin' at the moon." Chad tossed the covers aside and soon stood by Tim's side and, in an unaccustomed display of affection, put his arm around his shoulders.

"You're kind 'a worried 'bout us movin' ain't ya? I know what'll take your mind off that," Chad whispered in Tim's ear. "Let's sneak down ta the kitchen 'n have us a big slice 'a Ma's apple pie. If that don't do it nothin' will."

"This is one problem even Ma's pie ain't gonna fix," Tim's voice became husky as a lump rose in his throat. "I'm scared, Chad durned scared. I sure wish Chet was here, he'd know what ta do. What do ya think he's doin' right now?"

"Knowin' Chet, I'll bet he's got his boots propped up on the front porch rail of some plantation house 'n drinkin' mint juleps," Chad said enviously. "More 'en likely got one 'a them southern belles a waitin' on him hand 'n foot, to boot. Prob'ly had his pick 'a ten or twenty 'a the prettiest gals in town. Yes sir, I'll bet he's in hog heaven right now."

The fact of the matter is that Chet did have his feet propped up on a rail, except it was on the railway flat car, not a front porch. His mind wandered from his folks to Cynthia Harris. It had been forever since he had told her, "Goodbye," at least that was the way it seemed. He could still feel her tender kiss on his lips and the softness of her form as it molded into his. Taking her memento from his pocket, he held the heart tightly in his clinched fist

The train slowed to a snail's crawl then stopped completely. The continual stops usually meant that they were taking on more cars loaded with soldiers. At first everyone jumped up to see if they were finally reaching their destination, but now few even opened their eyes at the stops. This time was no different. Snoring filled the night air and Nate Caldwell was doing his share to add to the chorus. Chet watched as a non-com stopped at each car and spoke with the officer in charge. Keith Staten jumped to the ground and strode toward the front of the train. Chet judged that at least a half-hour passed before he returned.

"All you men that are awake, I want ya ta wake up the man next ta ya," he yelled. "I want everybody ta hear this, 'n I want every man ta stand up so I know everyone's awake." From other officers similar commands echoed down the line.

Chet shook Nate by the shoulder, but the only reaction he received was a grunt and the snoring resumed. Taking more drastic measures he placed a well-aimed kick at the sleeping man's foot.

This got results as Nate jumped to his feet, his fists clinched and ready for a fight. Holding his forefinger to his lips Chet pointed toward Keith.

"Men," Keith shouted, "the train is overloaded and the engine can't pull all these cars. There's a rough grade up ahead 'n the way things are now, we can't make it. Seein' as how our regiment 'n a few others ain't got no fightin' experience, they're gonna put us off on this sidin'. They'll send another engine from the next stop ta haul us on. We might have a considerable wait, so y'all make yourselves comfortable. That's word directly from the Colonel."

"That tears it," Nate grumbled as he hit his fist against the rail. "All the good stuff'll be picked over by the time we get ta the fightin'." Slamming his hat down onto the floor he kicked the side of the seat. Flopping down beside Chet he continued his tirade. "Should 'a joined the Union Army 'stead 'a this honey 'n biscuit outfit. Least I'd 'a gotten somethin' more out 'a' it 'en blisters on my behind."

"What are you mumblin' 'bout? What's that junk 'bout joinin' up with the Yankees anyhow?" Chet sat straight up on the seat, not believing what he had just heard.

"Look Sprout. In case ya can't figure it out for yourself, I'll spell it out for ya. Why do ya think I joined up with this bunch 'a no accounts anyhow? It sure wasn't 'cause I felt no patriotic duty or nothin'. The only reason any war's fought is for the booty ya get out 'a it. Same with the governments 'n same with me. Do ya think them Yankees are fightin' the south ta free a few skinny Blacks? Heck no. They's fightin' 'cause if they win, they get their way 'n can control prices on all the crops they can't raise up north, what's shipped to other countries. Ta be honest with ya, the South has 'bout as much 'a chance 'a winnin' this war as a grasshopper in a hen house. They's out manned, out gunned, out smarted and out 'a luck. We ain't got the steel mills they got up north, or near as many railways, or half the money they got."

Chet couldn't believe what he was hearing. This talk was nearly treason and he wanted nothing to do with it. It was beyond his comprehension as to why a man would join a war for personal gain. There seemed to be no pride in the uniform, or love of country as far as Nate was concerned, only personal gain. This thinking was unfathomable to Chet.

"Nate, I tagged along with ya 'cause I figured ya was a wise veteran 'a them wars in Texas. Are ya tellin' me that the only reason ya fought the Mexicans was for what ya could steal, 'n not for the freedom 'a your own home state?" His emotions made his voice raise and he was drawing the looks of others around him.

"If ya shout a bit louder they might hear ya back in Hannibal," a much-agitated Nate growled. Lowering his voice he continued. "Look Boy, I like ya 'n I admire ya for what ya believe in. As for me, I can't see myself getting' shot for no two-bits a day 'n feed. Down Texas way, we'd raid the Mex's villages 'n what goodies we could find 'n hide was ours. At first I was thinkin' like y'all, that it was all wrong. Then I found out that the Mex were doin' the same thing on their raids ta our side. So ya see, it ain't stealin' durin' war, it's the spoils of war that I'm takin'. Someplace I heard that some guy say, 'If ya don't take it somebody else will.' Don't ya see that if ya beat the tar out 'a the other guy, yer the victor 'n y'all are entitled ta takes what ya want." Nate's voice had taken on a nearly pleading tone, as he tried to convince Chet of his convictions. "There ain't gonna be no glory in us shootin' some young fellas what ain't even had their first shave yet. Just for the sake of argument, let's say the Confederacy won this war. Do ya suppose they'd be content ta just shake hands with ol' Abe 'n let bygones be bygones? Not on your brass buttons they would. They'd want their share 'a the spoils of war. They'd tell the Union how much they had ta pay for them tearin' up the land 'n damage they done. It's called restitution, 'n the only difference 'tween me 'n governments is I get mine first. I figure them fat plantation owners got plenty 'a silver in them drawers, 'n if I don't get 'em first some Blue-Belly will. Y'all don't want ta contribute ta the wealth 'a the Union, do ya? Anythin' them Yankee soldiers find'll go straight ta ol' Grant's army 'n that leaves us rootin' for acorns. No sir, I ain't gonna leave nothin' for that Union scum ta take, I'll get it first."

Chet had listened to every word that Nate had said. At first he had thought poorly of his companion, however the more he talked, the more sense it made. Why leave anything behind that would help the North beat them? As much as he tried to convince himself that what Nate had said was true, his Christian upbringing would not let him be a part of pillaging, especially from Southerners.

"Sorry Nate, I just can't buy it. Call it whatever ya want. Be it spoils, or loot, or just plain stealin', it's still wrong. I want ta end this war as bad as anybody, but I ain't gonna be takin' from folks that I'm fightin' for. Maybe the Yankees can use what I don't take, but that don't make it right for me ta steal it. Ya had me really confused at first, but I got thinkin' that Ma'd skin my behind for takin' somethin' that ain't mine."

"Ya got a lot ta learn 'bout war, boy. I'm gonna hate ta leave ya behind 'cause you're gonna be a lost child without me here ta lead ya along. Soon as they get this car on that there sidin', I'm gonna grab my knap 'n rifle 'n sneak onta one 'a them cars headin' out. You're welcome ta join me if ya wants, but this child's out ta here.

It's been 'most a month since the war started 'n I figure I already lost out on a bunch 'a stuff ta fill my knap with. Can't see wastin' no more time here when they's ripe peaches ta pick. Are ya with me or not?"

"I thank ya for lookin' out for me 'n all you done, but I guess this is one time ya got ta go alone. I couldn't look at myself in a mirror if I let myself become a common thief. Ya may look at things different 'n you're entitled ta your way 'a thinkin'. I reckon this is where we part company 'n I wish ya well. Ya been a good friend 'n I'll never forget ya, Nate Caldwell." Nate's huge hand engulfed the one offered by Chet. When the opportunity came Nate slipped over the side of the car and disappeared from sight. A deep feeling of remorse swept over Chet, for he knew this would be the last time that he would see this giant of a man who had befriended him.

There was no sleep for most of the men that were left behind when the engine chugged into the distance. Chet followed its progress by the clatter of the wheels against the steel tracks and the occasional whistle, then nothing but silence. He knew that when the sun rose there would be the customary head count and they would discover Nate missing. It was no secret that he and Nate were friends, so it was natural they would come to him first. Nate's words rattled around in his head like pebbles in a bucket. Chet still couldn't quite convince himself that Nate was either perfectly right, or perfectly wrong. His arguments were sound, but they flew in the face of everything that he had been brought-up to believe in. Stealing was against the Ten Commandments, which was God's law. If he would inadvertently aid or abet the enemy, he had broken military law. Would he be guilty if he didn't take things that would aid the Union? The tug-of-war was still going on in his head when the call for muster sounded. The troops jumped from the flatcar to form ranks and the vacant spot was very evident.

"Where's Caldwell?" One of the men behind Chet whispered. When Chet ignored the question, he received a jab from behind. "Hey Baxter, I'm a talkin' ta ya. Where's Caldwell?"

"Do I look like I sleep with Caldwell? How the heck should I know where he is?" Chet snorted as he turned and glared at the man. "Last I seen 'a him he'd gone ta the bushes ta do what comes natural 'n I ain't seen him since. Ya jab me one more time 'n I'm gonna shove that there rifle down your gizzard." Facing front again he felt some remorse for blowing up the way he had. After all, it was only natural for one soldier to wonder about another. He was about to turn and apologize, but silly pride prevented him from doing so.

"Adams," called out the Sergeant, the muster had begun. An answer from the back of the ranks and the noncom went to the next name and the next. Upon an affirmative answer he went down the list. "Baxter," Chet answered, as had the others. "Caldwell," the name rang in Chet's ears. No response, so he repeated, "Nate Caldwell," with still no response. "Has anybody seen Caldwell?"

"Seen him a headin' for the bushes sometime last night," Chet knew he had to say something, before he was singled out anyway. "He had a problem he had ta take care 'a, leastways that's what he told me. I went off ta sleep right after he did that, 'n when I woke up he wasn't back yet." The lie stuck in Chet's throat and he thought of Ma's eyes looking directly into his. He was always a lousy liar and he hoped that the guilt on his face wasn't too obvious to the Sergeant.

When roll call was finished, the Sergeant turned to Captain Harris. "One man missing sir. Nate Caldwell is absent and not accounted for." Keith and the Sergeant had a short conversation, and then the Captain stepped forward.

"We have no idea how long we will be stuck here, so we got permission ta set up down by the stream. Make yourselves as comfortable as ya can, but I don't want nobody leavin' the area 'less someone goes with. The rest 'a you men fall out 'n Baxter I want ta see ya." The tone of Keith's voice sent a chill down Chet's spine, but he did as ordered.

"Yes sir," he stammered. " What is it y'all want ta see me 'bout?" As soon as the words were out, he knew that it was an idiotic question. "If it's 'bout Caldwell, I done told the Sergeant everythin' I know," he hurried to make amends.

"Perhaps, ya can tell me too," the Captain's eyes narrowed and seemed to probe directly into Chet's very soul. "If he's run, he's put a black mark on the whole Missouri Eighth Regiment 'n I'm gonna bust my guts ta get him back. Now I want a straight answer from y'all 'n I want it quick. Did Caldwell run?" Chet looked at the ground and hesitated. "It's a simple yes or no answer, Baxter. Did Caldwell run?"

"No sir, I don't reckon that he run. Like I told the Sergeant, he had ta go so he headed for the bushes 'n that's the last I saw 'a him." Chet had convinced himself that Nate hadn't really run. In his mind, "To run," indicated that he had deserted and Nate had gone into the fight, not run from it.

"Okay Chet, you can join the other men, but I'm sure there will be more questions." Chet relaxed a bit as the Captain's voice seemed to mellow. "Oh bye the way, do you know the penalty for aiding any soldier to run? In case it has slipped your mind, the penalty amounts ta a long drop with a short rope around your neck. That's all Private Baxter, y'all are free ta go 'n join the others."

Men scrambled to find the choice spots along the stream and by the time that Chet arrived, there was nothing but leftovers. Some had already staked out their area and were frolicking knee deep in the cold water. On the banks shoving matches erupted, when one man thought another was infringing on his territory. Carrying his knap, rifle and bedroll, Chet located a place that well suited his needs. It was behind a tall bush and away from the main body of men. Brushing the ground clear of debris he spread out his blanket. Lying in a supine position he gazed at the blue sky, barely visible through the canopy of leaves.

"Ya done it now, Chester Baxter. Ya lied your way right inta a hangman's noose," he thought to himself. As he pondered his fate Chet barely noticed that the daylight was slowly slipping away. As far as he could figure he had three options. He could say nothing and stick with his original story, or he could fess up and tell the truth and hope for leniency, or he could do as Nate Caldwell had done and run. This army life was nothing like he had imagined it would be. He was homesick, lonesome and bewildered, as he became more unsettled by the situation. "Now I sure wish I'd 'a listened ta Pa 'n stayed at home," he thought. "Better still I wish I was sittin' home right now, a smellin' Ma's cookin' 'n listenin' ta Pa's whoppers. Bet they's just settin' at the table 'n finishin' a big slice 'a Ma's fresh baked pie, right now."

In actuality the rest of the Baxter family was just south of Perryville, Missouri. The dust from the lead wagon nearly choked

Tad, Chad and Tim as they pulled the neckerchiefs higher over their faces. Their parents had taken the lead in the newer wagon. The boys were left with the one Pa had traded for along with the pair of dun-colored mules. The rim was slightly bent on the right rear wheel, causing the wagon to sway slightly every time it made contact with the ground. A combination of the heat, dust and swaying had made Chad nauseous and he was constantly throwing up as he hung over the tailboard.

"Hey Pa," Tim yelled as he slapped the reins on the mule's rumps, "I reckon we'd best stop for a bit. Ol' Chad here's feelin' pretty poorly 'n Tad ain't a lookin' too good neither. Wouldn't do no harm ta rest these broken-down mules anyhow. They's lathered pretty good 'n the left one seems ta be favorin' his front foot." The only reaction he received was a wave of Pa's arm. The rough road stretched on and, just as he was about to make another plea, Pa turned his team into a grove of trees. By this time, much to Tim's delight, both of his biggest tormentors were draped over the back of the wagon. Pa stopped in a clearing that was bordered on one side by a slow moving creek. Pulling his team even with Pa's Tim climbed from the seat, while the twins moaned in the back.

"Don't reckon they's gonna die," Ma sighed as she checked the two, "just got a bit 'a ridin' sickness. Tim, y'all fetch some wood so Pa can get us a fire goin' 'n I'll brew some nettle tea ta settle their stomachs." Tim scurried to gather the abundant deadwood and soon the fire was blazing, the coffeepot full of water placed at the edge of the flames. Meantime Tim was investigating the occupants of the water. A small leopard frog stared back at him, as he lay on the cool bank, and tadpoles swam in the shallows.

"Pa, do ya reckon I could maybe get us some fish for dinner? I seen three or four in this hole 'n I bet there's plenty more 'round." Tim's exuberance, besides the fact that the lad had been cooped up in the confines of the wagon, made it impossible for his father to refuse.

"Don't see no harm," Pa nodded, "'sides, fresh fish might be just what we need. Just remember son, anythin' over twenty pounds ya gotta throw back." Pa chuckled at his own humor and went back to his fire, while Tim hurriedly cut a stout willow. A few yards of line tied to the end, a new hook from his box and a rusty bolt for a sinker and he was ready. Bait was no problem, as there were plenty of grasshoppers, and soon Tim was throwing his line into the water. He had no sooner cast than Pa brought the team of horses to the edge to drink.

"Pa, how come we gotta take all them back roads? 'sides bein' dusty, they ain't no towns or nothin along 'em?" Tim asked as Pa held the reins.

"Well son, I look at it this way. If them roads ain't much traveled 'n there ain't no towns, then there ain't no reason for any 'a them no-good gangs 'a deserters ta be here neither. I reckon they stay where they can get loot from travelers."

"Is it okay if I head downstream a ways? Ain't no use 'a me wastin' my time here with them horses a slobberin' in the water." Tim gave the animals a look of disgust. Pa simply nodded, as he lit his pipe, and Tim was off at a trot.

The willow covered bank made for slow going, however it also hid the fisherman from his quarry. Parting the foliage just enough to fit the pole through, he was rewarded with a fat nine incher that gave him a good tussle before he had it flopping on the bank. The farther downstream he went it seemed the bigger the fish got. Abandoning the willows, he walked along a game trail until he found a good pool to try. In the clear water a dark shadow shot from bank to bank. Dropping the line in he waited patiently. As he sat well away from the edge, he watched the grasshopper struggle on the end of the hook. Just as he was about to give up, the fish shot from it's hiding place and inhaled the luckless insect. The stout willow pole bent double, as Tim tried to keep from breaking the line. Running downstream, with the fish trying to get away all the while, Tim was continually slipping on the moss-covered rocks. Fighting to keep his balance, he continued until the fish finally gave one final jump and the line went limp.

"Dad-nab-it," Tim shouted at the departing fish. "I hope I gave ya one heck of a toothache, ya no good thing." Pulling himself up the slippery bank, he laid in the cool grass. He was resting from the exertion when the distinct sound of gunfire drifted on the breeze. He made out the unmistakable smaller pops of a pistol, followed by the booming noise of Pa's shotgun, and then silence. Dropping the fish Tim ran back toward camp. In the excitement to catch fish he did not realize he had traveled so far, until he was retracing his steps. The sound of pounding hooves on the hard-packed road made Tim redouble his effort. They couldn't be leaving him behind. Blindly he pushed through the undergrowth until at last he entered the clearing. In retrospect it seemed everything happened in slow motion. The willows parted to reveal a sight that would haunt Tim for a long time. Chad lay next to Ma, while Pa was slumped behind the wagon. There was no sign of the other twin, as Tim ran to his mother's side and bent over her inert body. Patting her cheek, sobs shook his frame as he gently cradled her head in his arms.

"Tim, over here," a voice called, barely heard above the water slapping against the bank. "Tim, help me." There was no doubt that it was Tad's voice coming from the willows. Running in the direction the sounds came from, Tim saw his older brother half submerged in the creek. "I been shot Tim. I done been shot." Crimson stains followed the water's flow as Tim pulled Tad from the creek.

"What happened," Tim managed between sobs, "Ma, Pa 'n Chad, they's all dead. Please don't y'all die on me too. I don't know what ta do, Tad." Tim watched as the red stain spread over the front of his brother's white shirt.

"Some fella came inta camp a wantin' a cup 'a coffee. Pa let him have a cup, then he whispered somethin' ta Ma 'n she came ta me 'n Chad." A wince of pain closed Tad's eyes for a moment, then he continued. "Ma told us that this guy was a Confederate deserter 'n ta run for it. He dropped Ma 'n Chad where they are 'n shot me too, but I crawled ta them willows. Pa grabbed the scattergun 'n the man shot him too, but not 'fore Pa gave him a load 'a shot. He got ta his horse but I don't reckon he got too far. The shootin' scared off our stock." Tad's voice began to trail off, his eyelids fluttering, as Tim held him close. "Reckon it's like Chet says, 'You're the man now.' Don't know what ta tell ya. If I was y'all, I'd be findin' Chet.'" He was still staring into Tim's eyes as he died.

Tim held the twin until the night chill and his wet clothes forced him to lay Tad back against the grass. The fire was down to but a few glowing embers and, using these as a beacon, Tim stumbled toward it. In the darkness he stumbled over Chad's outstretched arm. Picking himself up, he automatically apologized to his brother for kicking him. Once the fire was going again Tim went to the wagon and removed the all the bedding he could find. Reverently he covered each member of his family, saying a prayer for each as he pulled the blanket over them.

Daylight found him staring at the flames, for every time that he closed his eyes the macabre sight of the night before had etched itself on the inside of his eyelids. Digging the graves, burying the bodies and erecting crude crosses over them, took Tim most of the day.

Tad had been right, the killer had barely made it to the road when Pa's shotgun pellets felled him. He was a slender man, about the age of Chet, wearing the Confederate uniform. All the buttons, insignias and pins were removed, leaving only a plain gray outfit that appeared silly without the adornments. Tim was not gentle as he rummaged through the dead man's possessions, which amounted to a picture of a woman, one cigar and three dollars Confederate.

Rolling him from side to side, Tim removed the gun belt, shells, knife and pistol. A final gesture of hate, Tim spat in the face of the man who had taken his family away. Choking back tears he took from the wagon what he could carry on his back. Turning for a final look at the rock-covered graves, he walked down the dusty road.

"Ya ain't twelve no more, boy, ya just became a man, least ways ya are if ya want ta stay alive." He wondered if a man was allowed to shed the tears that were flowing freely down both of his cheeks. "Reckon it'll take a while 'fore I get ta be fully a man."

CHAPTER SIX.

While Connie and Ida were eating their evening meal the oval tubs were hauled into the kitchen. Placed back to back, offering a bit of privacy that way, they were filled with hot water and awaited the guests. True to her word, Ceil had taken personal charge of the preparation and had the top afloat with jasmine petals. The reaction of the hot water on the soft petals filled the kitchen with a sweet fragrance.

"Perhaps the trouble we went through getting here was all worth it," Ida commented as she put the last sliver of Ceil's cornbread into her mouth. "I have never eaten such wonderful cooking in my entire life. No wonder your grandfather prized her so much. That woman is the Rembrandt of the culinary arts. Where did he find such a treasure anyway?"

"I have no Idea where Ceil came from. As a matter of fact, I don't know anything about any of the servants here at Cyprus Wood." Connie was very careful to use the word, "Servants," rather than, "Slaves." Lifting the demitasse cup to her lips she sipped the molasses sweetened coffee. "I do remember grandfather saying that, 'He wouldn't part with Ceil for any amount of money.'" A rap, then the sliding open of the heavy oak door, interrupted their conversation. A man, who Connie estimated to be in his early forties, entered and slid the door closed behind him.

"I'm so sorry I am late but I was held up in town longer than I expected." Approaching the two ladies he made a slight bow. "I'm

Tom Judd. I'm sure that Mister Adams has told you about me and my duties here." Connie found the man very attractive and he carried himself like one who was very confident. The square jaw, deep blue eyes and curly brown hair, atop a muscular frame, made her almost wish that he were twenty years younger, or she twenty years older. One by one he gently kissed the backs of the ladies offered hands.

"Yes sir, I think I'm going to like this place just fine," Ida smiled as she looked at the spot where Tom's lips had barely touched. "Tell me Mister Judd, are all men in the south as much of a gentleman? If so, I have doubts of ever returning to Pennsylvania. Don't you think so, Connie dear?"

Ida's question made Connie flush a bit in embarrassment. He was indeed handsome, well mannered and also too young for Ida and too old for her to become infatuated with. Not used to Ida's ways, Tom was a little embarrassed also.

"I'm sure you find that all men in the south are pretty much as men anyplace else," he smiled as he dropped his gaze to the floor. "There are good and bad anywhere you travel. Southern gentlemen seem to have a reputation they must try to live up to. It's no different with southern women, what you folks from the north will call, 'Southern Belles.' Most northerners seem to expect us to be in a special class. Either whip wielding ogres, or pompous gentlemen who do nothing but sip julep all day and kiss the hands of beautiful women. I thank you for the complement, Mistress Ida. However I hope I don't disappoint you when I tell you that, like our counterparts up north, most of us are simply working to put food on our tables and keep a roof over our heads. To northerners our ladies are seen as all being beautiful queens, who parade around in gowns that would make European royalty look like paupers. While I will admit that the ladies in the South are more attractive than most, present company excluded of course,'" he quickly added, "most are as common as anywhere in the world."

"You covered that very well Mister Judd," Connie grinned, as he had quickly corrected the near blunder. "I'm certain that we will find things not much different here than they are at home. I hope I'm not being rude, but Ceil has set up tubs for Ida and I to bathe. We have had nothing but those small basins to wash in since leaving home, and we are in dire need of soaking in a tub. After your long day I imagine that you could use some relaxation also. If there is nothing pressing, perhaps you would join us for breakfast in the morning and we could discuss matters then. I have so many questions that you will probably be bored to tears by the time that I finish them all."

"Tomorrow for breakfast, it is," Tom agreed, as he bowed and started for the door. "Perhaps you should tell Ceil what time you wish to be awakened. Our day normally starts at six with breakfast. If that hour is too early for you, we can arrange for a later time. Just let Ceil know, she can tell me, and I will come down at your appointed hour."

"Six will be fine with us," Connie said hesitantly, for it had been a long time since her day had regularly begun at that hour. "We are not here to disrupt anything and we don't wish to throw your schedule off. We'll see you at six, Mister Judd." With another slight bow Tom walked out and gently closed the doors behind him.

"I'm sure going to look forward to that meal," Ida grinned. "With table decorations like that one, it will be a pleasure to get up that early. Don't you think so, Connie dear?"

"You embarrassing old coot," Connie grinned back, "he's out of both our age ranges. I swear that if you keep it up, I'll have Ceil fill your tub with ice water to cool you off."

"Look honey. This old figure wouldn't look good in one of those fancy Paris gowns either, but it sure doesn't stop me from admiring them," Ida gave Connie a sly wink. "I'll bet he has every woman in Georgia chasing after him."

"In that case he won't miss one less, because all that will happen between the two of us will be strictly business. Unless you have some other lurid remarks to make we could use a bath. I for one am going to take mine immediately. You may enjoy the smell of that train smoke, but I certainly do not." Connie arose and slid open the doors. She was startled when Savannah greeted her on the other side.

"Master Tom has told us that you are ready for your bath. All preparations are completed for you ladies and Ceil has personally taken charge of things. There are even extra jasmine in the water," she smiled. "If you would follow me I shall show you the way." A look of amazement passed between Ida and Connie as Savannah led them down the hallway and into the warm kitchen.

"I reckon everythin's ready for ya Miss Constance 'n Miss Ida." Ceil knelt beside each tub and plunged her elbow into the water to test the temperature. Nodding her head that all was well, she shooed everyone else out and closed the door. "You lady's clean stuff's on them chairs, right down ta your unmentionables. Got a woman servant outside ta keep everybody out 'n if y'all needs somethin', I'm right outside too." Ceil fairly bounced to the door in her haste to leave the two to their privacy.

"Please don't go, Ceil," Connie voice stopped the woman as she placed her hand on the knob. "There are things that I must know about Cyprus Wood. Please stay and we can chat while we soak." The servant woman turned and Connie could see the delight in her eyes.

"Yes ma'am, Missy Constance, ol Ceil she tell ya everythin 'bout this plantation. Ain't a whole lot goes on 'round here I don't hear 'bout." Seeing that the women had started to remove their clothing, she turned her back to preserve their modesty. "Y'all just let me know when y'all's in them tubs."

"You may turn around now, Ceil," Connie said, as she lowered herself into the tub. "Please pull up a chair and sit by me." Doing as she was bid, Ceil placed her spacious body in a chair by the tub and grinned at Connie. "First of all," Connie began, "I want to know about Savannah. Where on earth did Grandfather find such a prize?" The grin disappeared as fast as it appeared.

"Your gran'pappy didn't find Savannah. She belong ta Masta Tom. He brung her with when he come here." Ceil began to squirm in the fragile chair and Connie was afraid the thing would collapse under the weight.

"How did Master Tom come to get her?" Connie pressed the issue. "A slave like that must have cost a fortune, on the market."

"Missy, I love ya, I really do 'n I'd do most anythin' for y'all. Y'all's askin' this person questions that I ain't got no business talkin' 'bout. That's white folks business 'n ain't no concern 'a us slaves. Bein' from up north ya ain't accustomed ta the ways down here. They's things that even the highest house servant ain't 'llowed ta talk 'bout. What white folk do 'n don't do is the first. I reckon y'all best ask Masta Tom these kind 'a questions."

"I'm sorry I made you uncomfortable, that wasn't my intentions at all. That young lady intrigues me greatly and I should like to know more about her is all." Throughout the entire conversation Ida had been silent but now she spoke up.

"Would it be against your ethics to tell me about that handsome Tom Judd? I swear that man would turn every woman's head in Pennsylvania. Who is he, where does he come from and how did he end up at Cyprus Wood?"

"I'll tell ya what I can tell ya 'bout Masta Tom." The grin appeared once more as Ceil inched the chair forward. "He's a real gentleman, he is, 'n for a white man he's one 'a the handsomest I done ever seen. He gets more work out 'a field hands 'en most, 'n, like when Masta Ham was here there ain't a whip on the place.

Don't know 'zactly where he came from, out west somewheres. Tol' me once but I done forgot, some strange soundin' name. Him 'n Masta Ham was partners in some kind 'a dealin's. Don' know if I got all the particulars right, but when Masta Ham took sick he bought Masta Tom here ta help run Cyprus Wood. Run the plantation like it was his very own, after Masta Ham done died. That man can tell ya where every cotton plant 'n every bean's planted here, 'n who done put it in the ground. Never forget the night he come drivin' up ta the house in that old wagon with that chil' a settin' on the seat 'side him." Ceil hesitated, afraid that she was approaching forbidden territory. Pushing back the chair she busied herself picking up the clothes from the floor.

"Don't stop now, for crying out loud," Ida spouted, "I hate being left out on a limb. This is worse than reading a mystery novel and you find the last page has been torn out. For the love of Pete, what child?"

"Little Savannah, that's what chil'. Reckon I ain't hurtin' nothin' tellin' ya what I seen. That babe all wrapped in a blanket 'n sittin' right there on that hard ol' seat next ta Masta Tom. Not one squall come out ta that chil' all the time she there. Masta Tom, he brung Savannah ta the house 'n I done took care 'a her. Like my own baby she was. Masta Tom, he always a hummin' 'n a makin' faces at the chil'. He do love that little gal. Raised her like his own daughter, he did. Watched 'em both grow, I did. Masta Tom a full growed man when he come here, but he took ta responsibility what shaped him. When Masta Ham's health a started a failin' he send for Masta Tom. He come 'n stepped right in 'n took over."

Both women were absorbed in the story that they barely noticed the water had become less than tepid. Connie had her arms on the edge of the tub and her head leaning on her folded hands. When Ceil paused Connie asked her next question.

"Am I correct that Savannah is not a slave then? She certainly doesn't have the mannerisms, or the vocabulary, of a servant." Her prodding again made Ceil visibly nervous. She gathered a large muslin wrap from the chair and held it out for Connie to dry on, then one for Ida. As the women wrapped the warm cloth around them, Ceil said softly.

"I think maybe I say too much already. Maybe ya best get Masta Tom ta tell ya the rest. Sometime my mouth gets a goin' faster 'n my brain, 'n pretty soon I done say more 'n I should." Patting the women dry she held robes for them to put on.

"I don't believe that you have betrayed any confidences tonight, dear Ceil. It was my fault for asking in the first place, but there is something about her that pricks my interest. I shall not press you further and I thank you for a fine evening, now I believe we shall retire. Until I soaked in that tub I didn't realize how exhausted I was." Taking Ceil by her shoulders she kissed her on the cheek. "That's for remembering how much I enjoyed the jasmine petals in my bath."

As Savannah led them to their rooms and turned down their bed linen, Connie couldn't take her eyes from the young woman. A strange magnetism drew her to this nebulous creature, one that she could not explain. Even her status among the house servants puzzled Connie.

"Savannah," Connie finally ventured the question that had bothered her since first seeing the girl, "how did you happen to come to Cyprus Wood? Your demeanor and speech is not one of an ordinary house servant, nor is your dress. There is something very special about you and I can't quite put my finger on it." The smile on Savannah's face disappeared and Connie wondered if, perhaps, she was walking on forbidden ground. "If I am being too personal, just tell me to mind my own business," she quickly added.

"You are the Mistress of Cyprus Wood and what ever you wish to know, I must tell you. No slave would dare to tell the master to mind his own business. Exactly what is it that the Mistress wishes me to tell her?" She stood by the bed; her eyes cast toward the floor, in a position, that Connie took to be one of submission.

"First of all, you are aware that I am from the north and I do not believe in slavery. From what I have been led to believe, I have complete authority to do as I wish with Cyprus Wood Plantation and all the property, including those in bondage. I do not look upon you as a slave, nor do I want you to feel as a slave. It is my intentions to sign letters of emancipation for every one that has been in servitude here, from house servants to field hands. There will be no more slaves at Cyprus Wood." Connie paused to let her statement sink in then continued. "If you are uncomfortable with my question, it is your prerogative to answer or not to answer. I would like you to look upon me as a friend, not as a foreigner who has come to be Mistress of this plantation." Savannah looked into Connie's eyes, as if to determine if what she was hearing was true.

"I would value your friendship greatly, however you had best hear about me before you decide on such a bond. Here in the south, and much of the north also, I am what is considered a non-person. My father was a Buffalo Soldier stationed in the western part of the country, and my mother was a white woman. They were traveling alone when Indians attacked them and both were killed. Master Tom found me beneath the overturned wagon. After burying my parents he raised me as his own. Indians had killed his own wife and daughter a few years before. Just before Master Ham died, Master Tom brought me all the way to Cyprus Wood. I believe that he raised me to take the place of the one he had lost. Because of my mixed blood I could never be considered either white nor free, so I have lived here in a state of limbo."

"I have never heard of the term, 'Buffalo Soldier'. Was it a special group that hunted for meat?'" Connie asked as she took Savannah's hand and sat her beside her on the bed. "If this is making you uncomfortable, you may stop at any time."

"I don't mind," Savannah continued, "it is a situation that I am forced to live with and nothing will change it. The Indians gave black soldiers the name of, 'Buffalo Soldiers'. They had never seen a black man before and the close cropped kinky hair reminded the Indians of the hair on the head of the buffalo, hence came the name. It had nothing to do with hunting. Master Tom has been like my own father to me. He made certain that I could do everything that his own child would be able to do. There was no color separation between us what so ever. On Cyprus Wood I am looked upon as the daughter of the master. Off Cyprus Wood, I am just another black that has been taught too much for her own good. I hope you don't consider me too forward if I offer you a word of advice. Perhaps you should discuss your plans to free everyone here with Master Tom before you make such a bold move. There are many ramifications that perhaps you haven't thought of. As for my story, that is about all there is to it."

"You have lived a very complicated life my dear, and I thank you for sharing it with me. What you are, and what you have been, makes little difference to me. I would still value your friendship, that is if you will have me as a friend." Connie held Savannah's hand tightly as she gazed into the dark eyes.

"I would cherish such a friendship greatly. Perhaps, next time you could tell me of your life? I imagine it is far more interesting than my own." Savannah returned the squeeze as she withdrew her hand from Connie's. "It is late and you must be up early in order to have breakfast with Master Tom. I shall awaken you in plenty of time. Goodnight and sleep well." With that she arose from the bed and walked to the door.

"Savannah," Connie said, "would it be out of order for you to join us for breakfast in the morning? There is so much that I need to learn, and I can think of no one that I'd rather have teach me than you." The smile broadened as Savannah nodded in the affirmative.

"I would like nothing better than to have breakfast with you. Master Tom and I usually dine together, but we weren't certain how you would feel about eating at the same table as I, so we decided to forego the usual meals." The door closed behind her and Connie crawled between the covers of her bed.

"Her story makes her even more interesting than ever," Connie thought as she blew out the candles and lay back on the feather pillow. "I wonder just how she would be accepted in Martindale, Pennsylvania?" The rasping sounds of the crickets soon lulled Connie to sleep.

Sunlight poured into the bedroom, as the heavy drapes were drawn open and Connie stretched and yawned. "Good morning Sav...", she began to say, but it was not Savannah who had entered her room but another woman servant.

"Ceil, she say for me ta come 'n wake ya 'n tell ya that Masta Tom's a waitin' for y'all in the dinin' room," the thin girl mumbled, half frightened at being in the presence of the new mistress. "She say not ta bother a dressin' 'n ta just throw on a robe 'n come on down." Handing Connie the dressing gown, the girl backed out of the room and shut the door behind her.

Stepping into the hallway Connie was met by Ida, who was just coming from her own room. Together they strolled down the stairs and entered the dining room. The deep furrows between Tom's eyes and the tear-streaked face of Savannah told them immediately that something was amiss. They sat holding hands, while a newspaper lay open on the table, before Tom.

"Please come in ladies," Tom said, rising from his chair in a gesture of respect. "I'm afraid that we have some news which may complicate matters here at Cyprus Wood, and the whole nation for that matter." Connie and Ida sat in the chairs as Tom pulled them out, then returned to his own seat. Savannah was dabbing at her eyes with a handkerchief as he continued. "I'm afraid that we are now at war with the northern states. Last evening Confederate troops fired upon Fort Sumter, South Carolina. Now a state of war exists between the north and south. Whatever plans you had for Cyprus Wood will have to be put on hold until this is over. My suggestion is that you return immediately to Pennsylvania. I shall go into Rome today and see about finding some kind of accommodations for your return."

"Does this mean that we are virtual captives here?" Ida asked huskily. "I had a feeling that something was wrong when we had to change trains at the Virginia line. When that Confederate officer was so concerned about Yankee spies, we should have turned around and gone home then."

"It's too late for recriminations now," Connie said. "What will happen to the people here at Cyprus Wood? As I mentioned to Savannah, I have plans to emancipate every one of them. I have no use for slaves, nor do I believe in selling a human being. I had planned to have everything wrapped up and return to Martindale within a weeks time."

"Savannah has mentioned your emancipation plans and I must caution you on such a move. I hesitate to use the comparison, however these people are like wild animals that have been raised in captivity. They have been fed, clothed, taken care of and nurtured all of their lives. If you suddenly throw them back into the wilds, they have no survival instincts and most of them will perish within the first few months. While they all look forward to being set free, to them it's like chasing rainbows. Freedom is just out of reach and something they only dream of."

"We all chase rainbows at one time or another," Connie argued. "Everyone wants something that is just out of reach and the only way to get it is to try. I would like to give these people an opportunity to make it on their own. If necessary I will give each one some money to start a new life with."

"I don't know how to make you understand," Tom said in frustration. "Let me put it to you this way. Even in Pennsylvania I suppose that you had a pet of some kind? Say for the sake of argument, it was a small dog. You took care of it, fed it and everything else one does with a pet. One day you decide that you no longer want to care for that dog, so you take it out into the country and drop it off to fend for itself. For the first few days, or even weeks, he survived. He must compete in a strange world with other animals for food, shelter and other things that sustain life. He is unused to hunting for food, so he eats what he can find lying around.

He becomes weaker because the native animals know how to take care of themselves, and they have no pity on a starving stray. Eventually he gives up and dies, not because of anything that he has done, but because he was simply ignorant of the ways of the world and you saw fit to set him free. This may be a poor metaphor, however you must understand what you would be thrusting these people into. You are the Mistress of Cyprus Wood and the decision is yours and yours alone. All that I can do is advise you. As for giving every slave money to help him or her start out on their own, it would be folly. They have never had money and have no concept of how to use it. The first sharpie that came along, would con them out of the entire amount."

Connie understood the situation that she was in, but the solution was indeed like the rainbow and just beyond her grasp. Her intentions seemed sound, before Tom Judd had muddied the water with the reality of the end results. The only sound in the room was the ticking of the grandfather clock, as everyone waited for Connie to speak. All eyes were on her as she drummed her fingers on the tabletop.

"If I leave Georgia now, what will happen to the slaves on this plantation?" The word, "Slaves," stuck in her throat but in fact that was what they were. "My grandfather left me the responsibility of this plantation and I feel a moral obligation to fulfill his wishes."

"As of last night there is no more Cyprus Wood Plantation, nor any other in the south. It is only a matter of time until we are engaged in our own fighting right here. You asked, 'What will happen to the slaves here?' Many will run off, only to die by the hands of slave runners, or some natural or unnatural causes. Some will stay here but, whichever the case, our way of life is nearing its end. The day will soon come when the glorious and proud South will be reduced to ashes. I made a vow to Hamblin Garner to look after his domain for as long as it existed. I shall keep that vow as long as I possibly can, however I will not put my daughter in harms way.'"

"Daughter?" Connie repeated, "But I thought…"

"Savannah is my daughter. There is more to kinship than any blood ties and as far as I'm concerned, no child from my own loins could be dearer to me than she is. My first concern is her safety and well being, while second is this plantation. I didn't pull her from that overturned wagon only to lose her to some senseless war. If necessary, I shall take her back west where her color is less of an issue than it is here."

This responsibility and dilemma was too much to be thrust upon the shoulders of anyone, much less those of such a young woman. Connie was perplexed and wished that grandfather had passed on this problem to Aunt Phoebe and left her the mules instead. "How long do you figure we have to do what must be done here?" Connie inquired, hoping for some solution to her problem.

"I'm afraid that we have already waited too long. When I was in town yesterday, I learned why the bank would not forward money to your account in Pennsylvania. They have already traded in all of the Union money for Confederate, and they have halted honoring any Union currency. Your bank would not honor Confederate money and, as of now, there is no rate of exchange between the two. There is no market for land sales, because the economy is so uncertain and everyone is hesitant to buy land that may be confiscated later. I'm afraid you own a parcel of land that is your headache and, short of abandoning it, no way to get rid of it."

The hole was growing deeper by the moment, as Tom painted a darker picture with every word that he spoke. The money that she and Ida had brought with them was totally worthless. The land that she wanted to sell was equally worthless and she had a multitude of slaves to look after. Her world began to crumble about her and she was powerless to do anything to stop it. This was not at all how she had pictured her arrival at Cyprus Wood.

"May I ask, what position you will take in this war, Mister Judd?" Ida's voice broke the silence. "It seems you are in as much of a trap as Connie is. On one hand you have a daughter of color, which you must rightfully protect. While on the other, you have an obligation to Connie and the promise to her grandfather. I may be putting it very bluntly, but how are you going to handle your own situation? Are you going to cut and run at the first opportunity?"

"I have already explained my stand. As long as there is no danger to Savannah, I shall stay. At no time will I abandon you ladies and leave you to the mercy of the unknown. I will offer you the same protection that I offer my child. It will be up to you to decide whether to take it or not. My parents settled in the Utah Territory when it was no more than a sterile wilderness. We had hardships there that would rival what the south will face soon, and I will not put Savannah through that. Planting crops only to lose them to some unforeseen forces, and the starvation that follows, is something that I will die to protect my daughter from. According to the newspaper the Union has started a blockade of the southern ports. That will mean that few ships will be able to run the blockade to deliver cotton and tobacco to Europe. That also means that there is no market for crops, so there is no reason to grow them. Farms will shrivel and eventually the food supply will dwindle. It may take some time, however if the war lasts very long you will see a demand for food that no longer exists. I will go into Rome today to see what the consensus of opinion is there, and about getting you ladies tickets back home."

Untouched except for the coffee, the large breakfast sat on the table. The grease from the pork chops began to solidify as they cooled then grew cold. No one was in the mood for food, only for a solution to the problem that was confronting them at that moment. Ceil must have been alerted to the situation, for she cleared the table without any comment then disappeared into the kitchen again. Tom Judd also left the room, leaving a somber trio of women to ponder their fate.

"It may only complicate matters," Connie broke the silence again, "but would you have Moses hook up the buggy, Savannah? I would like to have you take Ida and I on a tour of the plantation. If I have an idea of what I have to deal with, it may help me decide what to do. The only memory that I have of Cyprus Wood is the way it was when I was a child. I'm sure that I will see it through different eyes now."

Wiping her eyes Savannah left to do Connie's bidding, while the two other women went upstairs and dressed. Connie met the others and together they walked silently down the stairs and into the entryway.

Moses was waiting for them as the three walked out of the front door. The peacefulness of the place made it hard to believe that but a few miles away, a war was raging. The coo of mourning doves filled the air as Moses drove the buggy down the lane toward the interior of the plantation. Passing fields of nearly ripe cotton and still sprouting tobacco plants, they wound their way past the houses where the slaves lived. Not much had changed in the past ten years, as Connie recalled each place in her memory. The buggy continued on until they came to where the road ended against a heavy cover of brush. Just as Moses was about to turn the buggy around Connie stopped him. Climbing from the seat she turned and surveyed the vast scenery surrounding them.

"Tell me Moses. How would you like it if I were to set everyone on this plantation free? No longer would there be any slaves on all of Cyprus Wood Plantation. Everyone could live here as free people and live their lives as they wished." Connie was hoping for a different answer than the one she received.

"Missy Constance, me 'n Ceil, we's too ol' ta be doin' nothin' but what we's doin now. We ain't knowed nothin' 'cept bein' house servants, 'n wouldn't know how ta be nothin' else. Same's with most 'a the others here. They jus' dumb folks what ain't got no sense when it comes ta thinkin' for themselves. We all been tol' what ta do for so long, that it's all we know. Don't reckon none 'a us really wants ta leave Cyprus Wood. That's the only worl' most 'a us ever know."

"Thank you Moses," Connie said as she returned to her seat in the buggy, followed by Ida and Savannah. "I believe that I may have a plan where everyone wins," she said turning to Ida. "It will all depend upon what Tom finds out in town today. Let's go back to the house Moses, I have some figuring to do." The rest of the ride was made in near silence and Connie's mind was so preoccupied that she barely noticed when the buggy pulled to a halt before the steps of the mansion.

"I done got some lunch ready for y'all," Ceil greeted them as she waddled out of the door and down the steps. "Y'all didn't have no breakfast 'n not eatin's not good for the body. Got some chicken 'n dumplin's, cornbread 'n fresh churned butter a waitin' on the table. Ya best hurry 'fore I throw it out ta th' hogs. Moses, ya shiftless no good, get yer body down 'n help them ladies." Moses grumbled something under his breath, but did as Ceil had told him.

"That chicken smell delicious," Ida commented as they entered the dining room. "I didn't realize how hungry I was until I smelled the food." The three made short work of the meal and were discussing the morning ride when Tom returned.

"The news is not too good," he said solemnly as he dropped into a chair. "There appears to be no train travel anywhere. The government has confiscated all of the railways to haul troops to where ever they are needed. All roads are blockaded while they search for any Yankee spies that may be trying to slip back to the northern lines. I'm afraid that you and Ida would have a very difficult time explaining what a pair of obvious northerners is doing so far into the south. They are questioning everyone with the slightest sign of a northern accent. The only reason that I am left alone is because I am well known in these parts."

"Couldn't you drive us to the border and, once we are across, you could return here?" Connie asked. "I realize that it would be a long and difficult journey for you, but I would make it well worth your while. We can't stay here forever, even if we wished to do so. We have our lives to live in Pennsylvania, not here in a place we don't even know the first thing about."

"I'm afraid that you are both victims of circumstance, my dear. What your grandfather believed was a legacy that he was leaving you, has become your own millstone. Around Georgia I am well known as the overseer of one of the largest plantations in the state. Outside of here I am just another man with a slight northern accent. I'm afraid that if I should attempt to deliver you to the border, we would all end up having to prove we are not spies. No thank you Constance. I prefer to take my chances here. With any luck the fighting will never get this far south and we will be safe here." Tom began to devour the plate of chicken that Ceil placed before him, when he raised his head and looked at Connie. "One other thing. There was a run on the bank in town and they closed it down. Everything you now own is what you see here at Cyprus Wood.

There is no money to buy anything with, and no hope of ever getting any back. You are rich in slaves, cotton and tobacco, but no money. I look for the army to confiscate what they need to feed the troops, so I wouldn't count on any livestock remaining around here to feed us."

Stunned, Connie sat silently. Her world was dissolving a bit at a time and it seemed that her destiny was in the hands of a far greater being than herself. She could not stop the tears that flowed, nor did she try. It was a woman's right to cry when she wished, and Connie certainly wished to do so right now.

"If you would excuse me, I am going to my room. There are a lot of things that I have to work out in my mind. I hope you don't think I'm being rude, but I need to be alone for a while." The walk upstairs seemed much longer and the stairs steeper, as she dejectedly strolled to her room. Once inside she fell across the bed and burst out crying. These were not the small tears that she had shed downstairs, but great sobs that racked her body. When there were no more tears left to shed, Connie wiped her swollen eyes and looked at the canopy over her head. The faded maroon velvet draped over the bed, held in place by the four walnut corner posts, was losing its sheen, much as life in the old south was. She remembered sleeping beneath this very same cloth years ago, when her only worry was if she could get Moses to carry her piggyback again. The soft knock at her door was almost as though the one on the other side was hesitant to disturb her. Before she could answer, the door opened a crack and Ida stuck her head in.

"Are you alright, Connie?" The concern on her face caused Connie to begin to cry all over again.

"Why do things have to be so complicated?" She said between sobs. "This place should be almost like a Garden of Eden, instead it has become a purgatory. It's become a place where we are stuck between two worlds. I thought things would be so simple. We could come here, enjoy a relaxing month or two and return home. I apologize for getting you into this mess, but I need you now more than I ever have before." Ida sat beside her and dried the tears from her cheeks.

"Look Honey. I've been through quite a bit in my time, and that Man upstairs has never let me down yet. Him and I have a regular talk every night come rain or shine. Most of the time He lets me work things out for myself, but I can see His hand in many of the solutions to the problems. It may be a small thing, like a subtle prompting, or directing me to what it is that I need to do. I don't remember anytime that He has dropped the answer in my lap. It's our job to work this out. I guarantee you that the Lord will have a hand in delivering His children from this lion's den also. Now dry the rest of those tears and let's go down and have a slice of that pie that Ceil made." Taking Connie by the arm, Ida led her back into the dining room.

Savannah sat at the table alone. Her eyes as red and swollen from weeping as Connie's were. Her hands were shaking as she dabbed at the tears with the linen handkerchief. She stood as Ida and Connie entered the room and made the curtsy that all servants are expected to do. Taking Savannah by the shoulders, Connie held her close.

"You don't have to curtsy to us. You are not a servant nor do I want you to feel as one. From the looks of things, there will be no more masters and servants separation here anyway. Unless things change dramatically, it will be total chaos instead." As they sat, the women picked at the pie on the plates before them. Eating the pieces, but not really tasting the sweet fruit filling, they were absorbed in their individual thoughts.

It was Ida who finally broke the silence. "Is your father gone again?" She inquired of Savannah, as she gave her a reassuring pat on the hand. "Things must be very difficult for him, having to take care of this place and especially under these circumstances. He is a very special person, and danged good looking too," she added with a grin.

"Ida, you're incorrigible," Connie said, as both the others laughed at her forwardness "There are times when I wonder if you don't have the morals of an alley cat. That station-keeper at the border advised me to keep you on a short leash, and he didn't even know you."

"That fresh mouth twerp," Ida retorted, "needed to have his behind kicked up behind his ears and tied there. As far as my morals are concerned, there's not a thing wrong with looking, even at my age. The day I stop looking you had best dig that deep hole and drop me in, 'cause I must be dead then."

"Master Tom has gone with Moses to the slave quarters. It seems the word of the war has filtered down and the slaves are restless," Savannah said as she nervously twisted her lace handkerchief. "He thought by talking to them he might settle things down. The last thing we need on top of everything else now is a slave revolt. I am worried though. This is the first time that he has ever taken a pistol when he has gone out to the fields."

"A slave revolt," Connie thought to herself. "Just another thing to worry about, as if there wasn't sufficient problems already." The look of concern on Connie's face made Savannah quickly add. "Like any place, there are a few hotheads and malcontents to contend with. While there is little danger of anything happening at Cyprus Wood, Master Tom thought it best to try to nip any problem in the bud. For the most part the slaves here are like children who need leadership. They look to the overseer for guidance, and only when that falters will there be problems. They admire and respect Master Tom, so I believe that everything will be all right."

The next hour, or so, was spent in idle chat. Ceil occasionally entered to refill the coffeepot, or bring in a steaming plate of pone and honey. She was lighting the candles on the table when Tom entered, followed closely behind by Moses. The expression on Tom's face indicated that there was something going on, while the grin on the black face spread from ear to ear.

"All right you two," Savannah said. "What have you been up to? You're glowing like a house afire and Moses is grinning like he's ready to burst. You haven't looked this way since you found out that Miss Connie was coming." A look of embarrassment took the place of smugness on Tom's face.

"Well, if you must know," he began as he sat in the chair next to Connie. "I went to the slave quarters and told them exactly what to expect. I figured that some would run underground, but that would leave less for us to worry about. I also mentioned that the banks were closed and the only money we had was what was left on the place. They would have to ration what supplies we have because we are unable to buy more. When we left, old Moses here asked me if we had money, would it help us? Maybe Moses had better finish the story, after all he's the hero in the whole matter."

"Ain't really nothin'," he began, proud to be the center of attention. "When Masta Tom talked that we needed money, I just knew where some was is all. Long time ago, when this fuss first started, Masta Ham he gets ol' Moses one day 'n tells him ta grab a spade 'n ta fetch th' wagon 'round. I did what he tells me 'n he gets me ta help tote out this here box. Not very big, but it sure heavy 'nuff that it near takes two 'a us ta pack it. He drives ta th' oaks 'n tells me ta start a diggin' a hole, so I does what he tells me. When he figures th' hole it deep 'nuff, he has me help put that there box in the ground 'n cover it up. He tells me this is for when times get bad, 'n I reckon times ain't gonna get no badder, so I tells Masta Tom 'bout it 'n he digs it up. We's here 'n there ain't no more ta tell."

"Moses is right, 'There ain't no more ta tell.' Do you think we should show the ladies what we brought home, Moses?" Tom said teasingly as he glanced at Connie. Moses nodded and the two men disappeared out of the doorway, only to return carrying a small chest. Moses struggled as he lifted it onto the table. Opening the lid only slightly Tom put one hand inside then withdrew it, his fist closed around the contents. "If each of you ladies would be so kind as to put out your hands, Moses and I have a small gift for each of you."

Doing as they were asked, Tom dropped a gold coin into each of the outstretched hands. "Ham was smart enough to know that eventually this day would come and he prepared for it. This chest must have hundreds of gold coins, ranging anywhere from five-dollar gold pieces to twenty-dollar gold pieces. When all of the combined Union and Confederate currency won't buy a pound of butter, one gold coin will buy a whole wagon full. I believe that this calls for some brandy. Moses you grab Ceil, the bottle and six glasses. You and your delightful wife will join us in a celebration. If it wasn't for you, we would still be trying to figure a way out of this predicament."

Moses shuffled out of the room, muttering something about Ceil not being all that delightful, or something to that effect. When he returned with Ceil in tow, they all toasted their newfound good fortune. Connie poked Ida's arm and pointed upward.

"You were right. He did deliver us from the lion's den." The smile on Connie's face halfway disappeared when Ida answered solemnly.

"I'm afraid not yet, darling. He has only given us the tools to help us find our way out. The rest is all up to us. I have faith that the good Lord will show us the way, however we are still a long way from being out of this mess."

CHAPTER SEVEN.

"How could an afternoon that had started out so perfectly, suddenly have turned into such tragedy?" This was the question that continually ran through Tim's mind as he trudged down the dusty road. The weather was great, the fishing had been good and the twins had been hanging out of the back of the wagon throwing up.

Despite his feeling of guilt, for laughing at his two brothers, he couldn't help but smile at the thought of the two draped over the tailgate. He continued to follow the impressions, that stood out like a beacon, in the soft dirt. One horse and the two smaller sets of mule tracks dug into the road.

"T'ain't our horse," he said to himself. "That's a ridin' horse 'n too small ta be one 'a our plow nags. Must 'a belonged ta that no account deserter. Them mule tracks never get no more 'n four foot apart. Reckon Pa must 'a tied 'em together." The gun belt, which was way too large to carry around his middle, was awkwardly slung over one shoulder. The shotgun was really more weight than Tim wanted to carry, but it was the only weapon that he really knew how to use.

His mind went back to the first time that Pa had let him shoot the ancient double barrel. He had taken Tim to the field behind the barn and set up some boards for him to shoot at. Handing Tim the old Parker, he told him that all he needed to do was point it in the general direction and pull the trigger. He did just as he was told, however the recoil knocked him through the wall of the chicken coop. They ate chicken for three consecutive nights to salvage the ones Tim had landed on.

A movement just off the road and perhaps forty yards ahead caught his eye. Raising the scattergun he slowly worked his way forward. He was right, Pa had tethered the mules together and the reins were tangled in the heavy underbrush. Fighting against one another the two mules were thrashing to free themselves. With one pulling one way and the other pulling in the opposite direction, they were only tangling the reins worse.

"Whoa mules," Tim said softly as he approached the terrified animals. "Ain't nothin' ta be scared 'a, it's only me, Tim. Calm down you jug headed crow baits, behave 'n I'm gonna get ya loose." Letting the mules get accustomed to his presence, and all the while cooing soft words to them, he finally succeeded in quieting the animals. Leading the two he walked them to the road and back in the direction where they had made camp. "Long as I got ya, I might as well use ya. We's gonna hook up that there wagon so I ain't got ta carry all this stuff no more. 'sides, I ain't hankerin' ta ride on your bony back, no sir I ain't."

The return trip didn't seem quite as long as the one going the other way, and before long the wagon was in sight. Mentally checking off each item, Tim loaded everything he thought he would need into the back of the bed. Hooking up the mules came next and with a final look around, he clicked his tongue and slapped the reins against the rumps of the team. The shotgun slapped against his knee as they entered the road, but he didn't mind that was his security.

"Lead on there mules," he said as he gave them another slap of the reins, "'cause I ain't got no idea where we's goin'. Shucks, I ain't even got no hunch 'a where we is now. There's a town 'a Perry a ways back, but even what state that's in I got no idea. I reckon that if this here road starts somewheres, it's got ta end somewheres too, so we'll just find out where."

Actually, Tim was just about to enter the border between Missouri and Kentucky. A neutral state at first, Kentucky had chosen to join the Union while it's southern neighbor, Tennessee had joined the Confederate States. Raiding parties from both sides constantly crossed the borders and harassed the troops on the other side. In an attempt to catch spies trying to infiltrate behind the lines, roadblocks were set up at every crossroad and bridge. Tim was barely across the line and into Kentucky when he had his first encounter with Union troops. Rounding a curve in the road he was confronted by eight armed Union soldiers. Pulling the mules to a halt Tim noticed two more in the trees on either side of the road with rifles aimed at him.

"Jump down from that wagon there tadpole," a man, wearing three stripes on his upper sleeve, demanded as he approached Tim. "What business ya got around here 'n what are ya doin' out here alone? Good night boy, ain't ya heard there's a war goin' on? You're liable ta get yourself shot roamin' around these parts."

Doing as he was told, Tim climbed down from the wagon seat and faced the soldier. Two others began to search everything in the bed. After they had ransacked everything they appeared satisfied and were about to leave the wagon, when one spotted the pistol lying on the seat.

"A might young ta be a Reb soldier, ain't ya son?" The man snickered as he held the gun belt up for all to see. "Reckon he's one 'a ol' Lees generals, do ya Sarge? Mighty shifty lookin' critter, I'll bet he's killed fifty Yankees with this here pistol." While everyone else laughed, Tim stood stoically. The laughter quickly died when Tim looked the soldier directly in the eye and said loud enough for all to hear.

"I took that there pistol from a Reb deserter what killed my folks. I let him have both barrels of that scattergun, 'bout tore him in half, it did." He continued to make the story better as he went. "I figured that 'long as he wasn't gonna need it no more, I might help myself ta his belongin's. Now if y'all don't mind sir, I'd appreciate it if ya would kindly put that there pistol back where it was."

Ignoring Tim completely, the soldier had taken the revolver from the holster, opened the cylinder and checked the barrel. He then checked the heft and balance of the gun before replying.

"Tell ya what there Button. How's about you givin' me this pistol as kind 'a souvenir? Always wanted me one 'a these Reb pistols 'n seein' as how ya got this scattergun, there ain't no need for ya ta keep this 'un." As he pointed the pistol at Tim a sardonic grin spread across his face. "What say Boy, is it a deal?"

Undaunted, Tim starred back. "'fraid I can't do that, mister. I done shot one man for it 'n I can't say I really cared for it much, but I hear it's easier the second time. Reckon I'll just keep that gun, so if y'all'd be so kind as ta put it back where it was, I'd be obliged ta ya."

"That sounded like a threat, ta me," the soldier said, a look of mock terror replaced the grin. "Didn't that sound like a threat Sarge? We best look out for this one. I'll bet he's midget 'n not a little boy at all. What do ya say ya little puke, are ya a midget?"

"I think you've had enough fun, Smitty," the Sergeant said calmly. "Put the pistol back 'n leave the kid alone. If what he says is true, he's gone through enough without havin' ta put up with some loud-mouth like you too."

Ignoring the Sergeant's words, the one called, "Smitty," was trying to buckle the gun belt around his middle, while holding the revolver in one hand. "Punch a hole or two 'n this'll fit me just fine. I sure do thank ya for this fine pistol, twerp."

"Smith, I told you to put that thing back where you got it. That's not a request, it's an order," the Sergeant barked, as his face grew red in anger. "You say one more word to this young 'un "n I'll have ya patrolin' the edge of the rottenest swamp I can find."

With much more force than necessary Smith shoved the re-volver back into the holster. Unbuckling the belt he threw it onto the seat and jumped from the wagon. Turning his back he muttered something that neither Tim nor the noncom could understand. Lean-ing against the rear wagon wheel he glared at Tim, the hate in the steely blue eyes was most apparent. Not intimidated in the least by the unspoken threats, Tim stared back until the Sergeant took him by the arm.

"Okay kid, let's get down ta business. I know ya ain't out on no Sunday picnic, 'n you're way too young ta be traipsin' around alone. For starters, where ya comin' from 'n what business ya got in these parts?" The once friendly voice had suddenly become ex-tremely business like.

Tim's mind raced as he thought of reasons this man would be willing to accept. If he ever needed to think up a believable whop-per, this was the time. "We never had a real place ta call home," Tim began. "Pa was a preacher 'n we traveled from place ta place so's he could save souls from Hell. We traveled all over, clear from

Illinois ta Texas 'n parts in between. Me 'n my brothers never had no real schoolin', 'cept for what Ma gave us. I just been kind 'a kickin' around since they got killed. Got odd jobs here 'n there ta feed me 'n the mules. Even had ta sell Pa's Bible somewhere's in Missouri, 'cause I got sick 'n needed some medicine. When Ma was alive she used ta give us herb tea for whenever we was ailin', but she wasn't there ta help me so's I had ta do my own doctorin'."

Casting a look at the soldier Tim tried to read the expression on his face. Uncertain if perhaps he was spreading it on a bit too thick, he continued. "Pa's cure for everythin' was good ol' Epsom Salts. He swore that they'd cure everythin' from a ingrowed toenail ta a ruptured eyelash. If ya hurt outside ya soaked in it, if ya hurt inside ya drank it." An involuntary shudder passed over him as he remembered how many times he was forced to take the horrible concoction, and the taste left in his mouth afterwards.

Evidently he was spinning a pretty believable yarn, for the Sergeant's arm suddenly went around his small shoulders. Even Smith had ceased glaring and was waiting on Tim's next word. No longer was he leaning against the wheel, but had moved closer so as to hear everything.

"When was it that ya had a decent meal son?" The noncom asked, his voice full of sympathy for the young lad before him. "We're just 'bout ta eat 'n there's plenty ta fill a small belly like yours. After ya ate ya can finish the tale. Ain't much, but probably better than what you had ta eat lately. Ya are eatin' ain't ya?"

"The mules stepped on a ground squirrel yesterday, so's I skinned it 'n cut away the bad parts. Weren't too bad eatin' once it was cooked good. I'd sure like ta have some good tastin' cookin' for a change, 'stead 'a roots 'n berries 'n greens. Even thought 'a shootin' one 'a the mules 'n havin' fresh meat, but I just don't hanker ta walk. 'sides couldn't kill one 'a Gods defenseless creatures just ta fill my belly."

"Smith," the Sergeant shouted, "seein' as how you're such a big man, you can take the watch while the rest of us grab a bite. Stop anythin' that comes along 'n if ya need help, just yell." Taking Tim by the arm he motioned for one of the other men to lead the team. The brush had been cleared from the roadside and a small fire was going. The familiar smell of boiling beans wafted from a pot hanging on a bayonet shoved into the ground. Blackened from much use, a large coffeepot sat on the edge of the flames. Taking a tin plate from the stack the Sergeant blew out the cinders and dirt, before scooping a large helping of beans and ham into it and handing it to Tim.

"You soldiers sure do eat good," Tim mumbled as he shoved a heaping spoonful into his mouth. "I sure hope my brother's eatin' this good, wherever he is." Accepting a cup of the strong chicory, he sat it next to him and took another mouthful of beans. "Name's Tim Baxter fellas, 'n I sure do thank ya for yer hospitality."

"You must be hungry ta think this stuff's good," one of the soldiers laughed. "'long as you're hopin', ya best hope your brother's got a better cook than we got. This guy takes the chicory grounds out 'a the pot 'n fries 'em up for breakfast, then he calls 'em pancakes. Where's your brother at, boy?"

"Can't really say," Tim said as he put the last of the beans in his mouth. "All I know is he joined up with the Union when Missouri went anti slave, 'n ain't seen or heard from him since. He sure looked proud a wearin' that pretty blue uniform." He then proceeded to relate how the rest of his family had been killed.

"Where ya headin'?" the noncom asked, as he offered Tim another helping of beans and more chicory. "Ya told us 'bout everythin' 'cept that."

"Don't really know 'zactly where I'm goin. Seein' as how my brother's the only one I got now, I'm gonna try ta find him." Tim tried to make his voice as pitiful as possible. "That was the last thing my Ma said ta me. I was ta find Chet 'n he'd look after me."

Pulling a letter out of the air, he hoped that there was a town that started with a "P" somewhere in Kentucky. "Last I heard was that his outfit was somewheres around a place that starts with a "P". It's a strange soundin' place 'n I can't never remember what it's called."

Each man tried to help him by naming off places that started with, "P". "Paducah," one volunteered, "Providence," another offered, while a third said, "How 'bout Pilotoak? That's 'bout as strange as they come."

"Where's these places at?" Tim asked innocently. "They all sound kind 'a familiar, but I ain't quite sure. Maybe if ya could tell me 'bout 'em, it'd help me remember the name."

"Paducah's just down the road a ways, but I don't think your brother's down there. Ain't heard 'a no outfit from Missouri movin' 'round here. Matter 'a fact, I ain't heard 'a no Union Missouri outfit a'tall. Might be Providence, but if it is ya got a long ride ahead 'a ya, it's north quite a ways."

"Naw, Providence don't sound right. What's the other one?" Tim hoped for one that was close to the border with Tennessee, where he could slip across and into Confederate territory.

"Pilotoak. That's south 'n east 'a here, but ya don't want ta go there. That's too danged close ta the Reb stronghold in Tennessee 'n they make raids 'crossed the border all the time," the Sergeant cautioned. "Maybe your best bet is ta head for Lexington. It's a far piece, but they got headquarters there that might help ya find your brother. Take this road for 'bout ten miles 'n you'll come ta a fork. Make sure ya take the one ta the left 'n it'll pretty much take ya in the direction of Lexington. The right fork'll head ya down ta Reb country 'n we sure wouldn't want that, would we?"

The rest of the time was filled with small talk. Not wishing to appear in too big of a hurry, Tim stood, thanked the soldiers for their many kindnesses and started to head for the wagon. A panic started to set in when one soldier leaned over and whispered something to the Sergeant. The noncom looked at Tim and nodded his head in agreement. The other man got up and walked toward Tim, who was ready to bolt at the first sign of trouble. Instead the soldier gathered some food, put it in a tote sack and laid it in the wagon.

"This'll feed ya for a couple 'a days," the soldier grinned as he patted Tim on the shoulder. "'sides, it's that much less our cook can ruin." Helping the boy into the seat he reached into his pocket and tossed him a four-bit piece. "Sorry I ain't got more ta give ya, Son, but ol' Abe don't pay his fightin' men much. Ya have a good trip 'n take care. Hope ya find your brother. So long." Slapping the mule on the rump he waved as the wagon jostled and bumped when it entered the road, he was then lost in a cloud of dust. "Good luck Kid. You're gonna need it. Ya got 'bout as much chance 'a findin' your brother as I got 'a makin' general in this here army."

"Ma's spinnin' in her grave at the whoppers ya just told," Tim said aloud, as he urged the balking mules into a trot. "Just ta get by sometimes, a fella just got ta stretch the truth a might. Do feel a bit sorry for them soldiers though. They's nice folk, 'cept for that Smitty guy. Thought for a while he was goin' ta get me caught." When he thought that he was far enough away from the barricade, he slowed the mules to a meandering walk. Letting them have their head he lay across the seat and whistled a tune that he had heard his mother hum. He could envision her humming as she went about her work at home. Rummaging through the bag of food Tim found six apples. Polishing one on his shirt he took a bite of the fruit, the sweet juice running down his chin. "Sure wish I knew 'zactly where y'all were Chet. Getting' mighty lonesome, I am. Shucks, I don't even know where ya were headin'."

At that exact moment, the two remaining members of the Lorenzo Baxter family were less than one hundred miles apart. Chet's company had been sent to Nashville, Tennessee to await orders. Both the upper echelon and Chet himself had long forgotten the Nate Caldwell incident. Rumor had it that the Eighth Missouri Regiment would be sent to reinforce General Pierre Beauregard's troops just north of Atlanta. His men had been engaged in the Battle of Bull Run a few months earlier. General Thomas Jackson had held his ground and the Union troops retreated all the way back to Washington D.C., however everyone knew that this would only be the first of such battles. The Union was gathering forces to launch a new assault on Manassas Meadows, where the small river of Bull Run meandered through.

"Never realized how much 'a chore this washin' is," Chet laughed as he pounded his spare trousers on a rock, then submerged them in the creek again. "No wonder Ma's always tired on Mondays. Washin' for six 'a us would tucker a body out proper." Laying his clothes aside he turned to the man next to him, who was rubbing sand into a stain on the knee of his trousers. "Ya scrub that there spot one more time 'n you'll wear a hole plumb through it, Dale. We been stuck here in Tennessee for too long now. How much longer 'fore we gets ta see some real action? I sure didn't join up ta wash clothes 'n set on my tail all day. Ain't no glory in what they got us doin'."

"Ain't got the slightest idea," Dale Parsons replied. Dale and Chet had been friends since they were both small and it was only by chance that they had found each other. Dale had left Hannibal the day after Chet and somehow the two ended up in the same regiment. "I heard that we could move out for Atlanta as soon as tomorrow, or as late as next week. I reckon that when they need us we'll go. Only complaint I got is the food. I figured they'd feed us proper, but this livin' off the land sure ain't proper. What ever we got for supper last night was sure bad. That meat was so old I bet he was around when Washington got elected president. Sure could do with some 'a Ma's pone 'n gravy right now." The conversation ended abruptly when the bugle sounded assembly and both men ran to answer the call. Most of the regiment was already lined up when they squeezed into their places. The company had nearly doubled in size since leaving Missouri. There were stragglers from other outfits, who had become separated from their own company, and a few volunteers swelled the ranks to forty-seven men all told.

"Men," Keith Staten shouted, "we've been told that a patrol of Blue-Bellies has crossed over from Kentucky and are raiding our blockades. We finally have a chance ta show the Confederacy what us Missourians are made of. I'm not shinin' y'all that joined us from other states too. We're ta scout the north perimeter 'n report back the enemy's strength. Make sure your rifles are cleaned 'n ready ta use if necessary. So we ain't so easy ta spot when we travel, we'll leave at sundown. This is what we been waitin' for, so let's us do it proud."

"Hot dang, "Chet exploded as he jabbed Dale in the ribs with his elbow, "I was just askin' for action 'n here it's handed ta us. By the time they were ordered to march the excitement among the soldiers reached a fever pitch. While the Sergeant counted cadence, rifles with fixed bayonets were held proudly at right shoulder arms. Every man's eyes were fixed solidly upon the back of the man's head in front of him. No one could deny that the Missouri Eighth looked sharp as they marched out of camp.

When after the third day of wandering in and out of fields, woods and swamps and no sign of Yankee patrols had been seen, the exuberance changed to grumbles. The meager rations had somewhat weakened the troops. To add to the misery nearly all of them suffered from severely blistered feet, which made every step a painful chore. The rifles were no longer carried proudly but in any happenstance manner that suited the barer. As they worked ever deeper toward the border the caution that was first shown, had been replaced by nonchalance.

"Rest here," Staten's voice carried back along the line of troops. They had come to another broad stream that needed to be waded. The men had come to hate these experiences for the boots became soaked, which caused more blisters on their already abused feet. Dropping where they stood the exhausted troops welcomed a rest of any duration.

"Baxter," the Sergeant called, "Y'all relieve Porter as the rear guard. He ought 'ta be 'bout four hundred yards or so back, 'n that's where I want y'all to be. If ya see a problem just shoot off a round 'n we'll come runnin'. I'll send ya a relief in a couple hours, 'til then keep your eyes open 'n your mouth shut. Understand?"

"Yes Sergeant, I understand. Four hundred yards back, keep my eyes open 'n my mouth shut. That's pretty much it ain't it?" A slight hint of sarcasm sneaked itself into Chet's voice. No one liked any of the point guard duty. A person was out there all by himself for hours on end. With no one to talk to it got terribly lonesome and every shadow seemed a threat. Grabbing his rifle by the barrel Chet backtracked down the trail. Just where the Sergeant had said he would be, Chet found Porter about four hundred yards behind the column leaning against a tree. He had taken the bayonet from the rifle and was scratching his back with its point.

"Bang," Chet shouted as he exited the trees and came into Porter's view. "Some lookout y'all make Porter. Ya'd be stone dead if I was a Blue-Belly. What a picture that'd make, when they found ya, with that bayonet down the back 'a your shirt 'n all. Sarge wants me ta relieve ya. They's all's up ahead at the edge 'a the stream. Looks like we gotta wade 'nother one 'a the blamed things."

"What Blue-Bellies ya talkin' 'bout? There ain't a Yankee in a hundred miles 'a this place," Porter answered in disgust. "Only Yankee here 'bouts might be that there bird that flew 'cross the border. I think they's just tryin' ta keep us occupied 'til the war's over. I wish there was some Yankees 'round here. Been so long since we shot our rifles, I doubt half 'a them'd work." With that Porter stood up and strode away, leaving Chet alone.

Sitting against the tree, as Porter had done moments before, Chet laid his rifle across his lap. As he thought of home the cool breeze over his perspiring body gave him a bit of a chill. He could hardly wait to be back and regale Cynthia with his war stories, even if they did have to be made up. Reaching into his pocket he removed the locket that she had placed there so long ago. Fondling the curvature of the small heart-shaped necklace he wished, now more than ever, to be home. He pictured him sitting with Cynthia on her front porch and hoping that her father didn't catch them kissing. Even though it was only in his imagination, he felt a flush of color spread over his face.

Engrossed in his thoughts, the first volley of shots coming from the river made him flinch. An even heavier barrage followed, then it stopped as abruptly as it began. Jumping to his feet Chet cautiously made his way back in the direction where he had left the others. Dropping to his knees, he pushed the rifle before him as he crawled through the heavy brush. His heart raced and his breathing became labored as he made his way closer to the river. Sweat ran down his forehead and into his eyes, blurring his vision until he could wipe it away. Crawling on his belly the final hundred yards, he parted the bushes that skirted the edge of the bank.

The carnage he beheld at that moment would remain permanently etched in his mind. Bodies were floating with the current to be carried downstream, while the banks on both sides were littered with soldiers dressed in Confederate gray. There was neither sound nor movement from either side of the water, except for the noise Chet made as he retched at the sight. Afraid to show himself he lay in the damp grass until he was certain that the adversary had indeed gone. Finally he dared walk among his dead companions. Keith Staten lay face down at the edge of the water, the back of his tunic a bright crimson. Struggling, Chet pulled him up on the bank and crossed the officer's arms over his chest. Keith would have no more use for his revolver so Chet reverently undid the buckle, and gently slid the belt from beneath him. As he backed away he nearly tripped over Josh Tate, the fourteen- year old standard bearer. He lay on his back, his arms and legs spread away from his body. His wide eyes staring at the trees above him, but now they saw nothing. A Yankee bullet had ended his life when it entered his forehead. The flagstaff lay just beyond his outstretched fingers however the flag, that he so proudly carried, was missing. No doubt now a souvenir of some Yankee, who would boast to his friends back home how he had taken it from a seasoned veteran in a well fought battle.

Even to Chet's untrained eye it was evident what had happened. The patrol that the Missouri Eighth was seeking had lain in wait on both sides of the river. When the majority of the Confederate troops were in the water and nearly defenseless, they were caught in a murderous crossfire. Retreating to the cover of the trees Chet stood bewildered as to what he should do next. It was obvious that there was nothing that he could do for the rest of the company. His own survival was foremost in his mind now and he knew that he must get as far away as possible from this place. Blindly he ran through the thickets back toward the road, to the spot where he had been sitting when the shots had first sounded.

Skirting the clearings and staying concealed by the undergrowth, Chet slowly made his way to the south. When dusk fell he walked down the very edge of the road, ready to jump into the cover of the brush along side at any sign of danger. A whippoorwill's call from the dense trees was the only sound, except for the shuffle of Chet's boots, as he cautiously moved along the rutted road. When it became too dark for him to see the road, he lay in the ditch by the side of it and pulled his blanket over him. Resting his head on his knap he fell into a fitful sleep. In his mind's eye the faces of his companions flashed one after another. He could picture them being cut down in a hail of Yankee bullets.

A combination of hunger pangs, terror and confusion awakened him before dawn. With barely enough light to see by, Chet resumed his trek. Through the trees the patches of shadows and moonlight on the road ahead played tricks on his eyes. He could almost feel the adrenaline pumping through his body as he crept along, searching every shadow for any sign of movement. A doe jumped from the thicket and crossed the road just ahead, giving Chet a fright like he had never felt before. The hair on his neck momentarily stood erect, as the deer disappeared into the brush on the other side. Chet plodded along uncertain as to where exactly it was that he was going, or if he was even going in the right direction. When daylight finally arrived he headed back into the dense underbrush to continue his journey.

The sun was just passed overhead when he thought he heard a rumbling of something coming down the road behind him. It was in the far distance and still indistinct, but Chet was certain that he had heard a foreign sound. As he lay hidden in the tall brush he cocked his head to try to hear it again. Waiting, he did hear it again. It was the sound that a cannon caisson would make as it was pulled behind a team. Perhaps it was Confederate troops, or perhaps it would be the Yankee patrol infiltrating deeper into Tennessee. Laying spare bullets on the ground before him Chet cocked his rifle and waited.

The sound grew closer and he could tell that it was a single cart or wagon, so he doubted that it would be a caisson. Waiting until the wagon rounded the curve Chet raised his rifle and was ready to fire, but then he saw that it wasn't any soldiers at all. A single man dressed in faded trousers and wearing an equally faded red shirt sat in the seat. His head bobbed to the rhythm of the wagon as it jogged closer. When it was nearly directly in front of him, Chet burst from the undergrowth his rifle raised.

"Reckon that's 'bout far as ya go, there mister," Chet said, a threatening tone to his voice. The one in the seat reached for a gun at his feet, but halted when he looked up at the soldier before him. Chet also lowered his rifle, a look of disbelief spread over his face. "Tim, is that you?" he muttered in disbelief. "What're y'all doin here, 'n where's the rest 'a the family?"

Tim rubbed his eyes, as if to erase the mirage before him. There could be no way that he had found his brother this easily, but fate had dealt him a decent hand for a change. "Chet," was all he could say as he jumped from the wagon and embraced his older brother. Tears ran down his face as he held Chet close, refusing to let go even when Chet tried to end the tight embrace. "Don't push me away just yet, Chet," Tim cried as he grasped his brother even tighter. "I kept hopin,' but doubted, that I'd ever see ya again. The rest 'a the family's all dead 'n I been travelin' alone for weeks. Didn't know where ta go or what ta do, so I just headed south 'n tried ta find y'all."

"Let's get this wagon off'n the road," Chet said as he finally released Tim's arms from around his waist. Leading the mules he found a place where they couldn't be observed from the road and stopped the team. Sitting Tim beside him Chet held his brother close. "Now, tell me all 'bout what happened ta the folks," Chet said, his voice husky as the lump rose in his throat.

Between sobs Tim related the entire story of Pa's deciding to leave Hannibal, about the encounter with the deserter and the meeting with the Union soldiers. Chet could feel the slender body shake beneath his hands as Tim finished telling about Cynthia's Pa and how she had left town.

"Ain't nothin' the same at home," Tim cried. "Gangs roamin' all over 'n killin' 'n burnin' folks out. Don't know if our houses's still standin' or if it got burned too. What'll we do now Chet? Sorry I let ya down, but guess I ain't quite ready ta be a man just yet. I'm scared 'n don't know what I'd 'a done if I didn't find y'all. I reckon it's okay ta be scared when you're young like me, ain't it Chet?"

"Age ain't got nothin' ta do with bein' scared," Chet answered comfortingly. "I don't mind tellin' ya that I'm plumb scared ta death, right now. I got no Idea where we are, 'cept someplace in Tennessee. Got no idea 'a where ta head 'n got nobody ta tell me." Chet related the killing of the entire Missouri Eighth Regiment and how he happened to be the sole survivor. "I reckon the first thing I got ta do, is find someplace safe for y'all ta hide while I figure a way ta join up with some other outfit. The ones on that train was headin' for Atlanta 'n I reckon that's where we ought ta go. If I can find which way it is ta Chattanooga, then we can head inta Georgia from there. If we keep the afternoon sun on our right side we ought ta be headin' pretty much south. I know for a fact that Chattanooga is south and west from here. Come mornin' that's the way we'll head, but for now we got ta find us somethin' ta eat."

"Shucks," Tim beamed, "eatin's no problem. We can eat courtesy 'a the Union army. Them soldiers at that roadblock gave me a whole sack 'a food. I got it in the back 'a the wagon. They's even a couple fresh apples in there." Running to the wagon Tim returned with the tote bag and he and Chet rummaged through it, shoving bread and pieces of apple into their mouths as they went.

"Next time ya see them Yankee friends 'a yours, be sure ta tell 'em how much we enjoyed the beans 'n salt pork. That was real quick thinkin' on your part, a tellin' 'em your brother was in the

Union army. Least ways it got us a meal or two out 'a it. Ya never did tell me how it was that ya found me clear out here. Must be thousands 'a square miles ta search 'n ya picked the right one. How did ya do that?"

"I didn't," Tim replied. "All I knew was that ya was somewhere in the Confederate army 'n with the Missouri Eighth. I reckon the good Lord had more 'en a bit ta do with me findin' ya." The smile disappeared from Tim's face and his mood became somber. "Tell me Chet, what's it like ta be in a shootin' war? Ya was so excited ta join up 'n have a chance ta shoot a Blue-Belly, but now ya don't seem the same."

Chet picked his teeth with a splinter of wood and leaned back against the ground. As if he was searching for an answer to Tim's question in the blue canopy above him, Chet looked at the sky. "When I joined up I listened ta all the talk 'bout the glory 'a fightin' for your beliefs, 'n how it was your patriotic duty ta give your all for the magnificent south. There ain't no glory in this war, or no other war. Just blood 'n heartbreak's all I seen. Met a fella back in the square at Hannibal that didn't want ta make friends. It was 'cause when they die he don't want ta cry for 'em. I figured he was a real loser until I lost a whole bunch 'a friends back at the river. Now I know what he was sayin'. When ya see 'em laid out 'n watch their life blood run inta the dirt, somethin' inside ya dies along with 'em. Nah Tim, there ain't no glory, or comfort, or pride in one man ta takin' another's life just 'cause some fat politicians can't agree. If war's so blamed important, why ain't they the ones out here gettin' killed? We're kind 'a like one 'a them pieces on a checkerboard. They move us here, 'n move us there, 'n when they get tired they climb inta a nice feather bed. When they gets hungry they head out 'n grabs a bite 'a hot roast beef 'n 'taters. All they's got ta worry 'bout's their puny reputations if things turn sour on 'em. Sure, they say there's a reason for this war. I'm just not sure if it's really a reason, or just an excuse ta force their way 'a thinkin' on ta somebody else." Chet hesitated as he looked at Tim to see if he really understood what he was saying.

"Geez, don't stop now," Tim blurted out. "I'm seein' a piece 'a ya that I ain't never seen 'fore. Are ya meanin' that Abe Lincoln 'n Jeff Davis are wrong ta start a war, 'n what's a reputation got ta do with it?"

"I'm thinkin' it's wrong ta turn a nation inside out just 'cause one side don't see the other sides ideas. It's just like a school yard fight. If ya stop 'n think 'bout it, they's mostly over some stupid misunderstanding. If the two guys just sat 'n talked it over there'd be a lot less bloody noses in town. So what if ya can't change the other fella's mind? All the talkin' in the world ain't gonna make no Methodist inta thinkin' like a Catholic, or a Baptist inta thinkin' like a Quaker, but does that make either of 'em wrong or right? Basically they all believe in the same God, it's when they start splittin' hairs they get ta disagreein'. When this shootin's over 'n they's writin' the history books for your grandchildren ta read, it don't matter now which side wins or loses. They ain't gonna remember the names 'a one 'a them men a layin' in that river. They's only gonna remember how that mighty President saved his country from tyrants, be it Lincoln or Davis. It'll be them that gets the glory, 'n the pride, 'n the bouquets of flowers throwed at them. If the one doin' the fightin' 'n dyin' even gets a decent hole dug for him he'll be lucky. They ain't a whole lot 'a glory 'n pride left ta a man, what's holdin both hands ta his belly ta keep his insides from fallin' through a hole made by a bullet, no matter what side he's on. Mark my words. When them books are written, it'll be that this here war was fought over the slave issue. That's only a very small part 'a the disagreement. The Union wants the Federal Government ta have control of any unwritten laws, while the Confederacy wants the States ta have that right. That's what started this whole mess 'n it's like a pickin' at a sore. Pretty soon it festers 'n never will heal, it just gets bigger."

"Y'all ain't planin' on runnin' are ya Chet?" Tim's face grew even more somber. "Are ya goin' ta be a deserter like the one what killed our folks? I always looked up ta y'all 'n tried ta be 'zactly like ya, but I don't know if I could handle ya bein' a quitter." Drawing his knees up under his chin, he clasped his arms around his shins and stared at his brother.

"I ain't gonna run 'n I ain't gonna quit. I gave my solemn oath ta protect the South 'n that's what I'll do. If I have ta I think I can even kill a man ta keep that oath, but that don't mean that I can't question the reason that I got ta kill him." Chet struggled with a way to make his younger brother understand. "Remember sometime back, when Pa sent me ta butcher a stewin' hen for supper 'n I killed that young rooster instead? Don't ya reckon that I knew the difference 'tween a stewin' hen 'n a rooster?"

"Sure do remember. Boy was Pa really sore at y'all for that one," Tim beamed. "Never gave much thought ta why ya done it, but sure was glad when ya did. That rooster was the meanest thing in the hen house. Hated ta even gather eggs out there."

"That's the reason he ended up in the stew pot. We all got pecked by that cranky ol' bird every time we'd go in there. Did ya ever stop ta wonder why he was that way?" A look of bewilderment crossed Tim's face and he shook his head. "We was goin' inta his territory 'n he was just tryin' ta protect what was rightfully his. That's a instinct what's born in every livin' thing, 'n I reckon that's why we're fightin' this here war. The Union's tryin' ta protect their way 'a thinkin,' 'n the same with the South. That ol' rooster never gave a thought ta who built that hen house in the first place, only that it now belonged ta him."

The two talked well into the night before Tim fell asleep and, as he had so many times before, Chet gently tucked him into his blankets. "Goodnight, little brother 'n I'm sorry that it had ta be y'all that had ta bury our folks. Ya might think that y'all ain't a man yet, but I'm not sure I could've done what you done." Bending, he kissed the freckled forehead then went to his own blankets. "I got ta thank ya Lord for leading Tim ta me, 'n now if ya could, please lead us out 'a the way 'a danger. I'm havin' a tough enough time just a keepin' myself in one piece. Amen."

CHAPTER EIGHT.

For Connie and Ida, what had begun as a week or two jaunt to Georgia had drawn out to nearly a year. The war raged on with each side winning skirmishes here and there, and occasionally a decisive battle or two. Like a huge game of tug-of-war the advantage went from one side to the other and back again. The Union troops would drive into the south, only to be driven back into their own territory. The loss of life was heavy on both sides and the fighting was no closer to an end than when it first started. Every day the Union sea blockade was taking a heavier toll on Confederate shipping. With no place to ship merchandise to, bales of cotton now sat molding on the platforms. The Confederacy had hoped for help from both France and England, the biggest overseas buyers of cotton, but none came.

As the demand dwindled the once thriving fields became overgrown with weeds. Once thriving plantation owners found themselves with masses of idle slaves. With the demand for southern crops dwindling, the market for slaves fell and they became more of a liability than an asset. Many were turned loose to fend for themselves, while others tried to run to the free states up north. Gangs of Blacks now became nearly as big of a threat as the Union army. By the cover of darkness they would raid plantations, steal what they could and burn the rest, leaving only death behind.

With their livelihood destroyed, or threatened to the point of extinction, many plantation owners formed armed groups that would scour the countryside. As a warning to others to not make the same mistake, any free-roaming Black would be suspect and immediately hung from the closest tree that lined the roads. For the ones caught there were no appeals. The innocent freed slaves met the same fate as the ones who ran.

While some of the surrounding plantations were destroyed Cyprus Wood sat as an island, unmolested and so far untouched. The orange glow of fires could now be seen almost nightly. Everyone knew it was but a matter of time before the raiders would come. Nightly, with his rifle in hand, Tom Judd sat on the porch and watched. One evening he was violently ill so Moses took his place watching over the house. This particular night a driving rain and cold wind never ceased and Moses contracted pneumonia. Nine days later he was buried in the oak grove, close to where his beloved master lay.

"It's just not going to be the same without Moses here," Connie wept, as they walked back to the buggy. "Things are getting darker by the day. It really doesn't look very good does it Tom?" Taking her by the arm Tom helped her into the seat. After helping Ida, Savannah and Ceil he walked around and sat beside Connie.

"I thought that when we found the gold Ham buried, it would be an easy matter for us to get you two out of here and back home. The back and forth battles have closed the all of the borders to the north up tight. It's way too dangerous to even try to sneak you out of here now. There is one way, but I'm not even certain that there would be absolute safety in trying it." Tom turned the team into the circle and stopped before the house.

"I gonna have some breakfast for y'all right soon," Ceil said between sniffles. "Give me a few minutes 'n I gets things a cookin'." The usually smiling face was haggard and her eyes red from crying.

"You'll do no such thing," Ida announced. "You will go to your room and lie down while I fix something to eat. When it's ready I'll call you and you will join us at the table." This came as a complete surprise to Ceil. Never was any house servant invited to dine at the same table as the masters. Looking to Tom for conformation or denial, she beamed as he nodded his head in the affirmative.

While Ida busied herself in the kitchen Savannah set the table, Tom and Connie sat discussing the future. "There may be a chance, a slim chance mind you, that we can head west and go north from there. A lot will depend on how the fighting goes, but right now it seems to be concentrated north of here." Pausing long enough to light a thin cigar Tom expelled the smoke toward the ceiling. "To be honest with you though, I'm not certain that there is anyplace completely safe. Those poor blacks are the ones I feel for. They're terrified that if they stay, the gangs of former slaves will think they are sympathizers of the whites and burn them out, or worse. If they run, the packs of whites will hang them for running. They are torn betwixt and between. Like most plantations around here our slave quarters are nearly empty. Most have hidden underground and the few left either have family ties that keep them here, or are too old to run. Unless something drastic happens it will only be a matter of time until we get hit." Savannah had now joined them, her brow furrowed in thought.

"Why couldn't we fix up the slave quarters and see if there isn't some way we could use them to house soldiers in?" She suggested. "We could use the spare rooms in the main house for the officers. Surely with a group of soldiers here the blacks would not dare attack us."

"That may be a solution, however it may also open us to an attack should the Union army come this far south. There have already been a few skirmishes in Atlanta, nothing major but still some fighting. Let me go to Rome later today and get a feel for what you have suggested Savannah. It may just work."

The conversation ended as Ida entered carrying a heaping tray of food, closely followed by Ceil. Hesitant to sit at the table with her masters she held back until Tom rose and pulled a chair for her. A mixture of gratefulness and embarrassment filled the ample body as she sat in the offered chair. Never had a white master done this for her, and she didn't quite know how to react to the gesture.

When the meal was over and they were sipping the final cup of coffee Connie broke the silence. "Tom, how far west do you think we would have to go before it would be safe to head north? It seems to me that before we were out of danger, we would have to travel though some pretty heavy populations of southern sympathizers. We can't go due north through Tennessee or South Carolina, as they are both strongholds of the Confederacy. Due west through Alabama and Arkansas isn't any better. It seems to me that we are trapped no matter which way we try to go."

"Connie's right," Savannah nodded, as she ran her finger lightly over the handle of the McNicol china cup before her. "There isn't much hope for us to leave. A man traveling with two Yankee women and a half-black servant can't get very far in this country. Everyone's afraid to get involved any more. If they should help a spy or a slave to escape, they would be hung for treason. I'm afraid that as far as getting us out of the south, all of Master Ham's gold won't do us much good."

"Perhaps," Tom agreed half-heartily. "Let me see what I can find out in town, then we can look at all the options. There must be a way for us to get you two back home."

"Us two?" Ida echoed. "How about the rest of you? Don't tell me that you are planning to stay here? There is as much danger to you as there is to Connie and me. I wouldn't feel right if you put your lives on the line just to protect the two of us. Savannah has as much to worry about as either of us. What about her safety?"

"We have already discussed that matter," Savannah said solemnly. "We are as well off here as we would be anywhere. In the north I may pass as Creole, or possibly even white. In the south there are so many of us with mixed blood that even the most inexperienced eye can pick us out. I have decided to stay behind. If any of you are caught traveling with a slave you will be suspected of attempting to smuggle me into free states. That could mean your life and I am not ready to accept that responsibility. The roads are crowded with vigilantes just looking for escaped slaves. Everyday more are caught and hung."

An uncomfortable silence filled the room as Tom pushed back his chair and left. Ceil busied herself clearing the table, while the other three sat trying to find a solution to the problem. The echo of hoof beats told them that Tom was on his way to Rome. Perhaps he would find an answer there.

It was late afternoon and Tom had still not returned. Ida and

Savannah had retired to their rooms and Connie sat on the veranda, watching the breeze ripple through the leaves of the trees. How could this peaceful setting be surrounded by a war that was taking so many lives? She remembered the carefree days in Philadelphia, when the biggest worry she had was which hat to wear to the theater. How things had changed.

"I hates ta bother ya Missy, but da y'all mind if I ask ya a question?" Ceil sat next to Connie, a perplexed look etched on her face. "Someday y'all's gonna be leavin here 'n leavin' me behind. Ceil's too blamed ol' ta be trapsin' all over, so can I stay here at Cyprus Wood? Promise ta take care 'a the place 'n not bother nobody, I do."

"You may do whatever your heart desires," Connie assured her as she patted the arthritic hand. "I imagine you have many memories of the plantation. I know that you and Moses are among my fondest memories of when I visited here as a child. You have been around for a long time, what do you think will happen to the south? So far we have been fortunate that the war hasn't caught up with us here. Do you think it will ever come here on Cyprus Wood?"

"Don' know what's gonna happen, Missy Connie. All I know's there ain't gonna be no winners in this fight. The south, she wins 'n...." Ceil stopped short and stared down the road leading to where they were sitting. "What the worl' is that 'n what's he doin' here? They ain't no dead folks here." Her eyes grew large with fright as she stood and backed toward the door.

Looking in the direction Ceil had indicated Connie saw a funeral coach, drawn by four matched coal black horses, turn into the lane. A large plume of black feathers adorned the top of the bridles of each animal, while the driver sported the customary black suit and tall hat. The brass oil lamps, on either side of the driver's seat, reflected the waning evening sun as the coach drew closer. Turning into the circle the driver pulled the team to a halt directly before Connie and a terrified Ceil, who was attempting to hide her huge bulk behind the much smaller girl.

"Did either of you ladies call for a hackney," the driver spoke softly as he raised his head to reveal a grinning Tom Judd. "What do you think of my new outfit? Imagine the looks we'll get when we drive this downtown Martindale. Just you, me and whoever we have in the back, huh Connie?"

"Thomas Judd, have you lost your mind?" Connie didn't know whether to laugh or throw something at him. "What in the world are you going to do with that thing? It gives me goose-pimples just to be so near it."

"I'm betting that most folks will feel the same way. This beauty is our way out of here. Take a look in the back for the rest of the surprise." Climbing from his perch high atop the coach, Tom opened the door at the back. Inside were two pinch-toe coffins of polished wood, with brass handles and carved edges. "Well, what do you think? Did I make a good trade or not?" The smile grew as he teased the women until Connie began to wonder if he really had gone mad?

"I must be slow but I don't understand. How are we using a dead wagon to escape, and what trade?" Connie searched his face for some hint of what was behind the broad grin.

"Masta Tom, this darkie don't know what ya got in mind ta do with this here thing, but one thing sure, ol' Ceil ain't gonna be no part 'a it. It's fo' haulin' dead folks in. This chil' done got a day or two 'fore I'se ready for that ride." As if the very presence of this black wagon of death was a bad omen, a visibly shaken Ceil stood as far away as possible. "If y'all don't mind, I got ta be findin' somethin' ta do inside." Both Connie and Tom laughed as Ceil nearly ran to the door and disappeared inside, then Connie turned to him.

"Is this some kind of macabre joke?" She asked. "I really do believe that you have been in the sun too long. Perhaps you had best come inside and lay down for a while." The concerned look on her face only made Tom's grin grow wider.

"This is no joke, my dear, this is a stroke of genius. I traded our buggy, the team of horses, my gold watch and Vulcan for this rig and I never had to touch any of the gold. The undertaker drove a hard bargain, but I eventually wore him down. I believe that it was Vulcan that sealed the deal."

"But Vulcan is your pride and joy, besides being the best piece of horse-flesh in the entire south," Connie interrupted. "How could you trade that magnificent animal for this?"

"A racehorse is a novelty that we can no longer afford, however this coach is. Let me put it away and tend to the horses, then I will meet all of you in the dining room. If you will have everyone there, I shall tell you of my plans." Climbing back into the driver's seat he drove toward the stable, leaving a bewildered Connie standing alone on the veranda.

As Tom had requested, Connie had gathered Savannah, Ida and Ceil in the dining room. They were sitting around the large table when Tom came through the door. Rolling down his shirtsleeves, he laid the black frock coat and stovepipe hat on the table and took a chair opposite Connie.

"Before everyone thinks I'm daft, let me tell you what I have planned. I had just arrived in Rome when the undertaker rolled the funeral coach out of the stable and was polishing the wheels. About that time these ladies walked by me and one of them happened to comment how that thing made her shudder whenever she saw it, and the others agreed. Then one said, 'How anyone could stand to have anything to do with dead bodies, is beyond me.' That started me thinking. Most people have a fear of corpses, so what better way to escape than by being one?'"

"That's it," Ceil said as she arose from the chair and beat a hasty path to the door. "This chil' ain't gonna play bein' no corpse, no time, no way. Soon 'nuff that ol' man death he's gonna be beatin' my door down, 'n I ain't got no mind ta hurry it along. Y'all can do what's ya want, but I'se gonna stay right here. T'ain't nothin' comin' what scares me more than ridin' in that there big black wagon out yonder."

"I suppose by now you have gathered that Ceil is definitely not leaving Cyprus Wood?" Connie smiled at Tom. "She was talking to me about it when you pulled up. It is her wish to remain here and spend her last days where she has buried her husband and I have consented."

"She has told me the same thing many times. She feels that she is way too old to be running all over the country and perhaps she is right. If she should change her mind however, we can always cram another coffin into the back of the coach."

Ida, who had been silent until now, pushed back her chair so violently that it nearly tipped over. "Connie has told me of that thing you've brought home. I'm with Ceil. If you think I'm climbing in one of those wood boxes, Tom Judd, you really are daft. I'll stay here with Ceil, thank you."

"Relax Ida. There is only one of us that will have to be in a coffin, and then only for a short while." Looking at Savannah the grin disappeared. "I see no other way to sneak you out of the south," he said almost apologetically. "I have worked this out to the smallest detail. Would one of you ladies please make us a big pot of coffee? I'm afraid that we may be in for a long evening while I explain it all."

When Ida and Savannah returned with the pot of coffee and a tray carrying cups, cream and a jar of molasses, Tom was busy drawing on a sheet of paper. Connie busied herself setting out the cups, while Savannah followed closely behind filling them with the strong black liquid. When everyone was once again seated Tom began.

"The way I see it, we only have three choices. We can head north, west, or stay where we are. There are inherent dangers in any of the three, but I'm afraid there is little we can do except perhaps to minimize them. I realize that you ladies want to return to Pennsylvania, but to do that we would have to travel right through the heart of some intense battles. I figure that if we can go northwest, through Tennessee and into Kentucky, we will be in free states. Once we are there Savannah will no longer have to hide and then we can plan our next move. It's a little over four hundred miles from here to well into Kentucky. Some of it through heavy Confederate strongholds, but I see no other way. If it looks like the war will be hitting the northern states, we can swing up through Illinois into Iowa and head west. Does everyone agree with me so far?"

When the only response he received were nods of the heads, he continued. "Savannah will be inside the coach, while the rest of us ride in the seat. We can pull the drapes so no one can see inside, but if we should be stopped you must climb inside the coffin and close the lid. I will have a Confederate flag draped over the lid and tacked into place. Just behind the three of us there will also be a coffin riding on top of the carriage. This also will be flag draped and we will tie rope through the handles and around the top rails to keep it from bouncing around. Ida, you will be the mother of two brave Confederate soldiers, who are the occupants of these coffins, while

Connie is your daughter. Your sons were killed in a train derailment when Yankee troops infiltrated and tore up the tracks. I will be the undertaker, and an uncle of the dearly departed, who is taking you and your beloved sons home to Paducah, Kentucky. Once we are out of Confederate jurisdiction we can dispose of the whole thing and do whatever necessary to get you where you want to go. Do you all understand the parts you are to play in our little drama? If there is any hesitation on anyone's part about your ability to carry this through, say so now. You must be convincing or all of our necks will be a bit longer than we are accustomed to."

"You forget one thing, dear Tom. We are women, and as such we spend considerable time convincing men that everything is not as it seems," Connie said, fluttering her eyelashes at him as she gave him a demure smile. "There is one flaw that I can see. What if we are stopped and they open the coffins?"

"I'm counting on them doing just that," Tom replied. "I will attempt to steer them away from the one inside the coach. However, if they do search the one that Savannah is in we are all trapped. I can't guarantee the entire plan, but I do believe that it should work."

"What will you have inside the coffin on top?" Savannah asked. "What makes you think that they will stop searching after opening that one?"

"That subject is a bit too harsh for the delicate ears of you ladies. Just take my word for it. Once they open that box I highly doubt that they will search further. There is always the possibility that I am wrong. If so, I deeply apologize and I shall see you ladies in whatever degree of glory that we go to. If anyone has another plan, please say so."

"You have never led us too far astray up to now," Connie smiled at Tom, "besides, I would hate to see you lose Vulcan for nothing. That brings me to another question. What makes you think that the undertaker in Rome won't turn you in to the authorities? After all, it isn't everyday that someone buys a funeral coach and drives it away."

"I told him that my uncle in Atlanta was also in the business, and that since the war started business was so brisk that he was searching for another coach. He hesitated at first. I simply pointed out to him that if he bet right Vulcan could make him more money in a day at the track, than he could make in a month at the parlor. Unless you ladies have anything else I believe that we should get a good night sleep. Starting tomorrow our days will be filled with nothing but preparations to leave."

As Connie tossed in the feather bed the night was filled with fitful dreams,. The sun was barely up when she was awakened with the feeling that she was being suffocated. Opening her eyes she found she had her head under the bedcovers to escape the overwhelming smell of boiling tar, which filled the room. Slipping into her clothes she went downstairs. Ida and Savannah sat in the dining room sipping coffee. Each was waving a fan before their face to eliminate some of the stench coming from somewhere outside and permeating the house.

"It got to you too," Ida commented as Connie sat at the table, "I near choked to death. It smelled like that pot was boiling at the foot of my bed. It sure gives this coffee a different taste."

"What in the world is going on, anyway," Connie asked as she poured her own cup of coffee. "If my guess is right, it's another of Tom's surprises. After last night I wonder what goes on in that devious mind. Who else would have thought of bringing home a funeral coach?"

"Devious, maybe," Savannah replied, "but definitely brilliant. That mind has kept me safe since he found me and there's never been a moment when I have doubted him. Perhaps we should see what the master is up to now. Besides, the air outside can't be more stifling than it is in here."

The morning sun, shining through the prisms of the windows, cast kaleidoscopes of color wherever it happened to land. Connie rubbed her hand across the sill, almost caressing it as she opened the door. It wouldn't be too long before she would no longer be mistress of this once magnificent plantation, but simply Miss Constance Garner, of Martindale, Pennsylvania again. The thought of abandoning Cyprus Wood bothered her greatly. The mere idea of it being overgrown with foliage and consumed once more by vegetation, which her grandfather had fought so hard to beat back, nearly broke her heart. This was not at all what she had envisioned so long ago when Mister Adams Esq. had read the will. Already the house was showing signs of neglect and the once manicured fields grown over with weeds.

She was still standing with her hand on the sill, mesmerized by the reflections, when Ida slipped her arm around Connie's shoulder. "By the look on your face my dear, there is definitely something else bothering you. Is there anything that I can do to help?"

"I was just thinking of how my grandmother stood right here and told me that if I could catch one of these rainbows, that I could have any wish I wanted. I would spend hours chasing them around but when I opened my hand, they had eluded me again. When I was small I would dress up and pretend to be the mistress of Cyprus Wood and mimic grandmother. I am only thankful that she and grandfather didn't live to see their dreams fall into what this place will become. I'm afraid it won't be too many years before Cyprus Wood will be reclaimed by the trees and swamps. In time there will be no evidence it ever existed."

"I suppose we just picked the wrong time to be born is all. Somehow there never seems to be a perfect time. At least you do have some fond memories of Cyprus Wood and those no one can take away from you." Ida opened the door and guided Connie out into the crisp morning air. "Now let's see what Tom is doing to make such a stink?"

Ceil was stuffing more logs into the fire beneath the tar pot as the three women approached. Tom had a stick with a wad of cloth on one end. Using the giant swab to dip into the tar he spread a heavy layer inside one of the wooden coffins. Carefully he covered the entire area, paying particular attention to each of the seams. Backing away he would survey his work and then see a spot that needed more pitch, carefully he dabbed a heavier coat here and there. Satisfied that the interior was sufficiently finished he then turned his attention to the lid.

"I suppose that you have a good reason for gagging us all with this odor?" Connie smiled at him. "Somehow I just can't see Savannah laying in that goop. What are you doing anyway?"

"That one's for Savannah," Tom answered, pointing to the other coffin that was leaning against the far wall. "This one's for our special guest who will be riding on top and right close to us." Smearing the final touch of tar on the lid he wiped his hands on his shirtfront.

"I believe that should do it. Let's get this tar pot moved so these ladies can breath again Ceil." Running a long stick through the bale handle Tom and Ceil picked the pot up and walked it well away from the stable. "Once this sets up most of the odor will go away. Until then, I'm ready for a big breakfast and then I have some chores to take care of. Would you ladies join me in a big plate of eggs and ham? That is if we could intrude on Ceil to fix them for us."

"Don' know what that 'trude' word means, but if you's askin' if ol' Ceil is gonna feed y'all, I'se sure is. Jus' give me some time ta wash this tar off with some coal oil 'n I'll get right to it. Don't look like ol' Ceil's gonna be fixin' y'all too many more meals, so this breakfast's gonna be extra good."

While Ceil was preparing the breakfast the rest sat around the table and asked the myriad of questions that had come to mind. They were in such a discussion when Ceil appeared with a platter full of food. Before posing more questions to him Connie allowed Tom to soak up the last of the egg yoke with his cornbread. "There are a few things that I have thought of since our talk last night. Why don't we just use a wagon instead of the funeral coach to carry the coffins in? That thing will draw more attention to us than if we shot off guns as we travel."

"First of all, the roads are packed with wagons and everyone will be stopped and searched for contraband, if not by the Confederate army then by the Union. I plan on attracting attention to us, but by doing so I also hope that our very attempt to not conceal anything will work to our advantage. We will travel the main roads and in broad daylight, just as if we have nothing to hide from anyone. The lone exception will be when we leave here. We will leave before midnight and by dawn we should be well beyond where I am well known. When I lived in the far west I watched the Indians dress in the hides of various animals. They were crude imitations I admit, but it would allow them to stroll among the herds and pick off the choice ones with out alarming the rest. Hopefully our ruse will work the same way." Leaning back in his chair, Tom looked at the others present. "Is there anything else bothering anyone?"

"You seem to have everything well thought out," Ida commented. "I hope you don't think that we are doubting you in any way. It's just that we are all a bit apprehensive about such a journey. What happens if we end up in the middle of a shooting war? The way each side keeps pushing the other back and fourth one never knows where the boundaries are."

"There are no guarantees, only hopes and prayers. I shall do my utmost to get all of us safely out of harms way, however once we leave here we are in Gods hands." The genteel look disappeared from Tom's face as he continued. "In my attempts to find a way out, I neglected to ask each of you if you really wished to leave? In my selfishness Savannah has been my first concern, and I assumed that you others would like to leave the south."

"I would like to leave anywhere that there's conflict," Connie said softly. "I'm not certain that by leaving the south behind we will find conditions better at home. There is as much chance of the war hitting the north as there is of the Union invading the south. Your first concern is for Savannah's safety, which it should be, but what happens to her if the Confederacy wins the war? The slave issue may spread to Philadelphia and Boston. She would be no better off there than she is here."

"Master Tom has thought of that also," Savannah interjected. "After we deliver you safely home, we are going to take the farthest northern route back to my home. He has never felt comfortable away from the west and that is one place where we will both be able to be free."

"There is to be no more of that, 'Master Tom,' stuff,'" Tom said sternly. "I have told you before about that. I know it's hard to break old habits, however you are not indentured to anyone, so no man's your master. Now if there is nothing further, I would suggest that you ladies began to set aside what you need to take. Mind you that it will only be the bare necessities. We are going to be a bit crowded in our little home on wheels, so choose your luggage wisely. Have everything set aside so you can pack at a moment's notice. The Union army has been as far south as the outskirts of Spartanburg, South Carolina before they were driven back. I'm afraid that it's only a matter of time before they come knocking at our door and I prefer that we were not home to let them in."

"I don't understand, Tom," Connie said innocently. "If we are running towards the Union army, why are we running away when they come here to us?"

"For the most part the stories that I've heard are not pleasant ones. Looting, burning and plain murder has occurred on both sides when the enemy territory has been invaded. Rather than leave anything that the other side may use, or possibly purely vengeance, both armies seem to have a policy of leaving nothing standing once they leave. Perhaps they are merely tales, but I don't you want to be here to find out. Besides, this may be your only chance to ride in that shinny coach and talk about it later."

"Come, ladies," Ida said as she rose from the chair, "we have some serious choosing to do and I'm sure it's something that we will all have to labor over. I know that I shall have a hard time deciding what to take and what will stay. I would suggest that, because Connie and I are to be grieving family, we both wear black dresses. That is appropriate attire for funerals in the south, isn't it?"

Before Tom could answer the thunder of horses hooves coming down the lane made them jump. Running to the door Tom jerked it open just as a dozen or so men reined their horses to a halt before the house. Most were from town but a few Tom didn't recognize at all. They carried an assortment of weapons, from ancient dueling pistols to modern rifles. Stepping from the porch he addressed one of the men at the head of the group.

"What's going on Mister Russell? Is there a slave uprising someplace? We don't have any problems here, if that's what concerns you, but thanks anyway."

"I'm afraid that we all have bigger concerns than that Tom. We came to get you to join us. The Yankees are ready to move into Tennessee and it won't be long 'fore they march into Georgia. We're going to help General Johnson's men fight 'em off. Grab your rifle 'n what bullets you got 'n come on."

"I'm afraid not, Mister Russell," Tom said. "I have more responsibility right here at Cyprus Wood. I can't run off and leave these ladies with no man around to protect them."

"Hidin' behind a woman, are ya?" One of the group shouted. "I never figgered ya for a coward, Tom Judd. But I reckon there ain't no other name for a fella that won't stand 'n fight for his country."

"You may call me what you will, but I still won't join you. Just look at yourselves. Those guns are so old that I doubt half of them will even fire without blowing up in your faces. You will be going up against trained soldiers who are equipped with the most modern weapons available. When that time comes you would be much better off by staying here and defending your homes and families. This war was not of my doing, or of my choosing. I am not from this area and the only reason I am here is as a favor to an old man that all of you knew and respected. When Ham asked me to come here from my home in the Utah territory, it was to be only until Miss Connie could settle matters. Because of the war she has been put in the position of having a plantation she cannot sell. The army has taken over the trains, so she is marooned in Georgia. No gentlemen, I believe that you had best not count on me to join your group." With no further words the men turned their horses and rode away.

"What will this do to our plans?" Savannah asked Tom. "It seems we are trapped no matter if we stay or if we leave."

"This moves our departure date a bit closer," Tom answered, a worried look etched furrows on his face. "Midnight tomorrow and we must be ready to go. We'll go as far as Chattanooga and see what it looks like from there. If there's fighting to the north, we may have to cut across into Missouri and then north. Missouri and Kansas pose nearly as big a danger as Tennessee does. All of the gangs and deserters seem to have found a haven there. I'll be back shortly and then I'll need the help of all of you to load the coach." Picking up his rifle, Tom turned on his heels and without another word, left the women alone.

<u>CHAPTER NINE.</u>

While Savannah held the lantern Tom finished tying the rope through the handles of the coffin atop the coach. Testing each knot and giving one final attempt to move the box, he dusted off his hands before helping Savannah down. Taking the light from her, he opened the back door and checked again to make certain that the flag draped coffin inside was also secure. Tilting the lid to lean against the inside window he surveyed the interior.

"I believe that we are ready for you ladies to load your possessions now. We must leave room for Savannah to move around and climb into the box, if circumstances demand she must do so." Putting his arms around her Tom kissed her cheek lightly. "I'm so sorry that you must be inconvenienced so my dear daughter, but I'm afraid that the times are desperate enough to warrant it. Hopefully it will be for but a short while."

Once the women had left the stable Tom began to rig the four horses, taking particular care not to forget the black plumes atop the bridles. Checking and rechecking his own belongings, he packed away everything except the rifle and the pepperbox pistol. The rifle was hidden under the seat and the pistol concealed inside the tall black hat. With the top as crowded as it would be, he fervently hoped that he would never have to have swift access to either of them. Before placing the box of gold coins in the foot of the coffin where Savannah would be hidden, Tom removed a handful to carry them through, at least for a while.

Once everyone's luggage was safely tucked into every available corner Tom closed the drapes on the inside of the coach. It was now time for the inevitable goodbyes and the tears that must be shed on such occasions. As Savannah and Ida were led away by Tom, there was heartfelt sorrow at this parting. Connie was the last to hug Ceil; the ample body shook with sobs as she held her mistress closer. Both knew this would be the last time they would embrace each other.

"I'm sorry Connie," Tom said softly as he took her by the arm, "but if we don't leave now daylight will catch us before we're out of here." With a final squeeze, Connie pulled away and allowed herself to be taken to the coach. As Tom boosted her into her seat next to Ida her final few minutes at Cyprus Wood Plantation were close at hand. Taking his place beside Ida, he slapped the reins on the backs of the horses and the coach jolted forward. Ceil stood on the veranda waving a white handkerchief as they rolled past. By the light of the lantern Connie could plainly see the tears that rolled down Tom's cheeks.

The road led past the oak grove, where her grandparents and Moses lay buried, and through the ornate archway. Connie kept glancing over her shoulder until the lights of the plantation eventually disappeared from view. There was no conversation as they continued toward the main road leading to Chattanooga, each lost in their own thoughts of what they were leaving behind and what possibly lay ahead.

Connie looked at Tom's face, silhouetted by the light of the brass lantern on the side of the hearse. She imagined how hard it was for him to be leaving Cyprus Wood, for it was the end of a stewardship that had been given him by a man that he loved as a father. She remembered how he had told her of when he first met Hamblin Garner. Ceil's version was fairly correct, with a few additions and omissions. Tom had been prospecting out west and there had been considerably more prospecting than finding. Before long both his supplies and money were about gone. Arriving at Truckee Meadows he tried to find a job to build up his dwindling supply of cash. It seemed the entire valley was filled with down on their luck miners, who for a quarter would muck out the saloons or do other menial tasks. He knew that two-bits a day wouldn't do him any good; he needed some sort of grubstake. Counting every cent in his pockets he came up with exactly seven dollars and forty-eight cents. Seven dollars and forty-eight cents, his horse, pack mule, a few digging tools, an eighteen hundred thirty six "Texas" Patterson thirty four caliber Colt pistol and the clothes on his back, were the total sum of his earthly possessions.

Lured west by the promise of easy riches in the gold fields, he joined the massive migration. By the time he reached the Utah Territory he found nearly as many heading back home as there were going on to California. The stories seldom varied. There was no gold just lying on the ground waiting to be picked up by the sack full. Killings and claim jumping were daily occurrences, while one person in a thousand found anything worth bragging about. Many stopped to try their luck around Gate's Crossing and Truckee Meadows, but their sluice-boxes were continually clogged with heavy blue clay like material. Dejected, most left the territory to return home in defeat, or simply vanish rather than return in disgrace and broke.

Tossing a four-bit piece into the air he caught it and slapped it down on his wrist. Heads, he would wager the last of his money on the poker table, and tails he would head for home. Heads it was. The saloon directly across the street was as likely a place as any to try his luck at cards.

Pushing open the bat-wing doors he entered and walked to the plank bar on the far side. This place was the same as countless others that dotted the area. The same smoke filled room, the same rough-hewn bar and the same smell of unwashed bodies and cheap whiskey. Rather than rush into the game he stood and watched the four players at the poker table. One was a grizzled old miner, who was far too drunk to be playing cards, the second a buffalo hunter and the other two were questionable. Both of the latter seemed to be attired the way professional gamblers dress. One wore the slick vest and dark coat, which seemed to be the trademark of men who made a living of gambling. The other reminded Tom of the riverboat gamblers that he had seen on the Mississippi. His clothes were obviously tailored. The ruffled shirtfront and Panama hat seemed out of place this far west. His pants tapered into the knee high black boots. Both men seemed too slick for Tom's liking, so he simply stood and watched as the game progressed.

When the grizzled old miner finally passed out, the bartender unceremoniously dragged him from his chair and deposited him in a heap in a far corner to sleep it off. Watching each turn of the cards carefully, Tom thought that he noticed the one in the vest slip a card from the deck into his sleeve. It had all happened so smoothly that he questioned if he had actually seen the cheat. When he saw him second card the one in the Panama hat, he was certain. Just as the cheat reached out to bring in the pot the barrel of Tom's pistol slammed down on his hands. Cards and money flew in all directions as Tom dragged the gambler from his chair. Pulling up his sleeve to expose the hidden card, Tom shoved the muzzle of the revolver under the man's nose.

"I don't mind seeing a fella win at cards, but I sure do hate a cheat," Tom hissed between clinched teeth. By this time the table was surrounded with on lookers and "Panama Hat" was standing beside Tom. The angry crowd took the gambler outside and, after receiving a severe beating; he was dumped outside of town. Receiving a promise that he would be the guest of honor at a hanging should he ever show his face in the whole territory again, he departed quickly.

"I believe I really owe you one," the man in the Panama said. "My name is Hamblin Garner, and I thank you for exposing that sharpie. I must say that he was more than proficient at his trade. I pride myself on being able to spot a cheat, however that one was far too good for me to see." The two shook hands and Tom introduced himself. The buffalo hunter picked up his money, and what he figured his part of the pot was, and left to join the others at the bar. Gathering the spilled money from the floor Ham put it all on the table and shoved the entire pile towards Tom.

"Well Tom Judd, I do believe that you won this pot without even turning a card. If it wasn't for you that slicker would have it in his pocket by now. There should be close to three hundred dollars in that pot and you earned every bit of it. I believe that I've had quite enough of this place for one night. I'm staying in the hotel across the street. Would you care to join me for a drink in my room?"

That was the beginning of a hard and fast friendship that lasted through the years. Whenever Ham took the train west he would look up Tom and they would spend all the time together that they could. Tom used part of the three hundred dollars to grubstake another try at finding gold. A few months after Ham left to go back to Georgia Tom was sluicing in an abandoned claim. The heavy blue material, that so many before him had cursed, continually clogged the box. About to give up and move on he decided to find out just what this miserable stuff was. Sending a sample to the assay office he was more than surprised to learn that his worthless blue metal was actually high-grade silver. He worked the claim for another eight or nine months, before discovering that the excitement was more in the search for the riches than in actually finding it. Tiring of the daily drudgery at the diggings he sold to a San Francisco conglomerate, which paid him handsomely for the rights his claim. Once again he was doing what he really enjoyed, prospecting. Days on end found him in search of another source of silver. He was in the midst of this endeavor when he received a wire from Ham, urging him to please come to Cyprus Wood Plantation immediately.

A sharp jolt brought Connie back to the present. The seat on the coach was made for two people at the most and three crowded it a bit. The armrest dug into Connie's side every time they hit a rut or bump. The surrounding darkness hid the perpetual tears that she could not stop from flowing. Her handkerchief was already damp, as she dabbed at her eyes. She wondered why every time she had become so attached to someone, they were taken away from her? First losing her parents, then her grandparents and now Moses, Ceil and Cyprus Wood. She began to wonder if she would ever see her home in Martindale again? Everything seemed so unreal. The meeting at the attorney's home, the reading of the will and the thrill of being the heir to her grandfather's plantation. Although she had never let on to anyone, she had often dreamed of being the mistress that she remembered her grandmother being. Dressed in fine gowns, the fan hanging from her wrist and the procession of young suitors that would flock to her door. At least she had the adventure for a while, something that few nineteen-year-old girls have, and no one could take those memories from her. Her mind wandered back and forth between the days spent with her parents and the many young men that had courted her. Those were happy times, not at all like today when they were sneaking out like thieves under the cover of darkness. She wondered how Savannah was fairing, being bounced around in the dark recesses of the coaches interior?

Ida it seemed could sleep anywhere. Her snores occasionally brought smiles to the faces of the two sharing the boot with her. Her head rolled from side to side and she leaned with each sway of the coach, pressing either Connie or Tom into the armrest. Ida's initial thoughts had been of her early life, her husband and finally of how she had became a guardian to Connie. Eventually the sway of the coach pushed everything from her mind, except for how tired she was, and no matter how hard she fought it she fell asleep.

Dawn was only beginning to show color in the east when they turned onto the main road leading to Chattanooga. Connie could barely make out Tom's features against the morning sky. She couldn't help but smile at the way he was dressed and how different it was from his usual style of clothes. The stovepipe hat sat askew on his head and seemed to change directions with each bump. The collar of the black frock coat was turned up against the morning air, giving him the appearance of having no neck what so ever. He was definitely dressed the part of an undertaker, right down to the pair of white cotton gloves covering his hands.

"Another of life's quirks, she thought to herself. "Who would have thought that Constance Garner would be riding on top of a thing that they used to carry the dead? Certainly not Constance Garner, for she was terrified of death and anything to do with it. She even kept as far away as possible from the coffin tied behind her. Even though she knew there was no dead body inside, just the thought of what it was used for gave her goose pimples.

Ida stirred and attempted to stretch, but the narrow seat prevented her from getting a good one. "How far have we gone?" She asked between yawns. "No wonder they use this thing to haul dead people in, these seats are certainly not made for the comfort of living flesh. Would it be too much of an inconvenience if we stopped for a bit? My backsides are asleep as well as both legs. There's a little man is sticking needles in the soles of my feet and I can imagine how uncomfortable it is for poor Savannah."

"I was thinking the same thing," Tom replied. "We have been

on the road for a number of hours and need to give the horses a rest. We should be past the point where I'm known. As soon as I can locate a spot to pull away from the road we will stop and let Savannah out of the back. We can all use a little exercise and, while we're at it, see what Ceil packed in that basket to eat."

The sun was well above the horizon when Tom turned the team down a trail that branched from the main road. The dusty road wound through trees and hanging vegetation and was barely wide enough to accommodate the coach. At times the occupants of the boot had to duck their heads to keep from being swept off by low hanging branches. When he believed that they were well away from prying eyes he pulled to a halt in a clearing. Huge willow trees hung over the brook, that wandered in and out of the clearing then disappeared in a thick growth of brush. Climbing down from the seat he helped Connie and Ida down, then he opened the back door for Savannah. They all found some relief as they walked around to loosen the cramped muscles and stiff joints. They were barely out of Rome and still had well over three hundred miles to go, the very thought of it made Connie cringe.

"Is there no shorter way we can get out of Confederate territory?" Connie asked Tom. "I'm not complaining, mind you, but it must be as uncomfortable for you as it is for us. That seat was not made for three people to sit on, and poor Savannah closed inside that box with the drapes pulled. She isn't even able to see what's going on outside and I'm sure the air gets rather stale in there."

"I'm afraid not. I've gone over every possible route out of here and this is the best one. We may be uncomfortable, but at least we are still alive and free, so far," Tom added the last almost as an after thought. Leaving the women he began gathering sticks and clumps of dried grass. Before long a small blaze was heating the pot of water, while the occupants of the coach walked off still stiff muscles.

"Tea's ready," Ida announced as she lifted the pot from the fire and filled four tin cups with bubbling hot water. Handing a cup to each she sat with the rest as they discussed what lay ahead. The general consensus of opinion seemed to be that if they were stopped, it was Tom who would do all of the talking. "You've got us this far Tom and as far as I can see we're in pretty good hands. My only

147

regret in this whole matter is that my behind isn't a lot smaller so we'd fit better on that seat. Perhaps I should climb in that other coffin and leave the box to you and Connie." Laughing at her own joke, Ida stretched her legs straight in front of her. "What do you figure our chances are of getting out of the South? No fibbing, we are all adults and there is no reason that we should be kept in the dark."

"To be perfectly honest, I have absolutely no idea. We have four different factions to deal with and each could be as dangerous as the others." A look of concern, which Connie had never seen before, came over Tom's face. "We have the Confederate Army, the Union Army patrols, deserters from both sides and their gangs of robbers and cut throats, and we have marauding bands of run-away slaves. All of them are in addition to the regular highwaymen that plague every road and byway in the country. I wish I could tell you what our chances are Ida, but there's just no way to know. I'm afraid that our fate is in greater hands than ours. I only hope that He isn't too preoccupied with more pressing matters to keep an eye on these four lost souls."

"Amen," Connie said almost to herself. "Do you think the horses have had enough rest Tom? You know how the midday sun gets so hot. Perhaps we could travel before and after that and rest during the heat of the day."

"There's something beneath that bonnet other than a pretty face," Tom smiled and gave Connie a wink. "The horses should be rested enough for the next leg of our journey. I guess the big question is whether Savannah is ready to be closed back inside again?"

"Don't be concerned about me," Savannah answered. "To hear Ida talk I'm much better off than the three of you are. If I get tired I can simply crawl into the coffin and take a nice long nap, while you all are cramped into that seat. I'm ready anytime that you are."

After drowning the fire Tom helped the ladies, then turned the coach around towards the main road again. "Hang on tight ladies," he said aloud, "maybe in about three hours we will stop for the afternoon and start out again around six or so. I'm really surprised that we haven't seen any patrols or roadblocks by now. I'm wondering if maybe they have pulled them up to the Tennessee border. If that's the case, it doesn't bode well for us."

"What does that have to do with us?" Connie asked. "The fewer roadblocks we have to go through, the happier I will be. I have a definite fear of being confronted and searched by a bunch of rowdy soldiers who haven't seen a woman in heaven knows how long."

"I don't know as that would be all that terrible," Ida chimed in. "Matter of fact, it may be down right pleasurable." Throwing back her head she laughed heartedly, as Connie gave her a scowl and jabbed an elbow into her ribs.

Once he quit laughing at Ida Tom grew serious again. "If they have pulled the soldiers up that means they are either engaged in a war at the border, or there will soon be one. Either way it might mean that we have to find another way out. The only possible way, besides the one we are now going, is through Alabama, Mississippi and up through Arkansas into Missouri. That would add nearly nine hundred miles to our trip and there is no way that we could make it out of the south before winter sets in." As much as he tried to hide it there was a look of panic on Tom's face, which made Connie fear for their safety also. His jaw was set as he clinched his teeth. The usual soft features had become hard and lines of worry etched themselves into his forehead.

"Are we really in that much danger Tom?" Connie asked. She noticed the normally steady hands begin to show a slight tremble, as he held the reins between his fingers. "I have never seen you so upset. If you are placing yourself and Savannah in harm's way simply to get me and Ida out, please turn around and go back to Cyprus Wood."

"For Savannah and me things would be no safer there than the risk we are taking now. Because I have refused to take sides, I am a marked man in the south. If the rebels don't kill me for being a coward, the Yankees will shoot me as a sympathizer. Because I am a healthy young male from the north who happens to live in the south, I am suspect to both sides. I guess that you might say that I have joined Savannah and became a non-person. No Connie, I am doing this as much for myself as for you and Ida." His weak attempt at a smile did little to comfort Connie and she turned her attention to the road once again. She became less aware of her peripheral vision and concentrated on the backs of the four horses in front. Watching the bobbing of the horse's heads and the rhythm of their stride mesmerized her. So engrossed was she that she didn't even notice the wagon that was set crossways to block the road. A sharp intake of breath from Tom brought her back to reality. Looking up she saw a dozen Confederate soldiers, each carrying a bayoneted rifle, lined the road. Gripping the armrest she fought the panic she felt rising in her breast.

"This is it ladies," Tom mumbled. "Go into your act and please, for all of our sakes, make it convincing." Knocking on the back of the seat, as a prearranged signal for Savannah to climb into the coffin and close the lid, he reined in the horses just short of the wagon.

"Mighty strange way ta travel, I'd say," one of the soldiers commented, as he aimed a stream of tobacco juice at the bushes beside him. "Ain't never seen one 'a these things up close 'fore. Y'all don't mind if we just take a little peek at what you're carryin' in there do ya?" The men surrounded the coach and one held the lead team by the reins.

"We don't mind at all gentlemen," Tom said, his voice surprisingly calm as he spoke. "As you can see, we are taking these two poor lads home for burial. They are brothers that were killed in a train that the Yankees derailed. This is their mother and sister, and I happen to be their uncle. I believe that you will find all these papers in order. A letter from the commanding officer of the deccascd boy's company stating what had happened, and letters addressed to me at my funeral parlor. They should prove our identities and our mission. We are taking them to be buried with the rest of their kin."

Connie glanced at Tom from the corner of her eye. He had really thought of everything, right down to forged documents and phony letters. With a flourish she removed her handkerchief from her bosom and wiped away imaginary tears.

"My poor brothers. They believed so strongly in the cause of the south, and for that they gave their lives." As soon as she said it she wondered if perhaps she had gone a bit too far with her acting. Glancing at the faces surrounding them she was happy to see expressions of concern rather than suspicion were on many of them.

"What ya carryin' in that there box on top there?" A soldier wearing the stripes of a Sergeant asked, as he drew closer to the coach.

"Only the body of my oldest boy," Ida wailed as she buried her face in her handkerchief. "He would have been twenty three on the day after tomorrow. His younger brother is in the coffin inside. He was barely eighteen. Now there's only us two women left to carry on." As she took her handkerchief from her eyes, Connie was surprised to see how red and swollen they were, while the tears running down her cheeks were the genuine things.

"I think y'all better climb down so's we can have a look see up there," the Sergeant ordered. "How come y'all got them drapes pulled? T'aint nobody that usually rides in these things usually cares 'bout how dark it t'is. Cobb y'all help the ladies down, then y'all 'n Shirtluff check out what's in that box on top."

"I believe that would be a grave mistake sir," Tom said as he stepped down and stood beside the non com. "Both these men have been dead for several days and they won't be exactly roses by now. The one on top is in better condition than the other. That is why we have the other inside, away from where we may be offended by the occasional odors."

"We're soldiers mister, 'n the stink 'a death ain't nothin' new to none 'a us. If y'all just hand over them papers the boys'll do as they been told." Taking the packet of papers from Tom's hand he opened the large brown envelope and sorted through them. Looking at one of the addresses on a letter he looked at Tom. "What's yer name there mister."

"Thomas Monroe Judd," Tom answered, as the Sergeant thumbed through the papers, "as it very plainly states on that envelope in your hand. I own a funeral parlor and dry goods store in Atlanta and I am taking my sister and niece to bury these boys in their home in Kentucky. The army has taken over all of the railroads or we would have them sent home by train, which by the way would have been a lot less hassle for all concerned."

The two soldiers on top of the coach had pried the lid loose on the coffin. No sooner had they cracked the top than the pungent odor of putrefying flesh filled the air. Hurriedly they replaced the lid and pounded the screws in with the butts of their rifles.

"No doubt 'bout it Sarge. They's nothin' but a dead 'un up

here," the man named Cobb said as he leaned over the top of the coach. "The smell 'ud gag a maggot in there. Are ya satisfied, so's me 'n Shirtluff can come down now? Don't really relish 'a bein' up here with no corpse, 'specially one as ripe as this one."

"I am truly amazed," Ida sputtered, her eyes rimed in red and an occasional tear still trickled down her cheeks. "My dear sons gave their lives for the Confederacy and men in the same army defile their corpses by disturbing their coffins. Who is your commanding officer? I will certainly write him when we get to Kentucky and tell him of this shoddy treatment."

"Y'all won't have ta wait 'til ya get ta Kentuck ta write nobody. We got orders ta take everyone we stop ta him. He's camped just beyond them trees ahead 'n y'all can tell him personal." Handing the papers back to Tom he motioned for the wagon to be moved. "If y'all 'ud be so kind as ta folla' me, 'n don't do nothin' stupid like tryin' ta run. I got four 'a the best shots in the whole Confederate army here 'n they'd nail ya 'fore ya got twenty yards."

Once everyone was in the seat again the coach followed the troops down the road. "So far I believe we have done exceptionally well," Tom smiled at the two women beside him. "Especially Ida and those tears. You are quite an actress my dear. Even your eyes looked as though you had been crying."

"I was really crying you blamed fool. Before we left Cyprus Wood I soaked the corner of my handkerchief in onion juice. You try rubbing that stuff into your eyes and see if you don't shed a few tears too. I wasn't sure I was that convincing an actress. When you were so adamant about our lives depending on fooling everyone, I just used a drop or two to help me along. You didn't do so badly yourself Tom. When they opened this coffin the smell was so overwhelming that I nearly fainted. What in the world is in there anyway?"

"I knew that if we got stopped, they would certainly search the coffin. That day at Cyprus Wood, after we tarred the inside of this coffin, I killed a hog and put the carcass inside. I figured that in a couple of days it would be getting so ripe that no one would want anything to do with it. So far it has worked, now if we can be convincing enough to fool the officer in charge. You ladies are doing a terrific job. Keep it up and we will all be safe and sound in

Kentucky very soon."

As the Sergeant had indicated the camp was not far, in fact just around the next bend in the road. Just below the lip of the trail neat rows of canvas tents lined either side of a large clearing. In the center were the remains of a fire-ring, where an occasional wisp of smoke could still be seen rising from the burned logs. Rifles set like tripods stood between the tents, the bayonets pointing toward the leafy canopy overhead. From her vantage point high above the ground the multitude of soldiers reminded Connie of a disturbed ant bed, with men seemingly going everywhere, yet nowhere in particular. Some hauled water from a broad river, while others dragged logs to the fire-pit, still others were busy cleaning the area of debris. A pair of brass cannons sat at either end of the camp, a keg of powder and a pile of balls beside each. The coach was taken down a well-worn trail leading from the main road and into camp. A gasp escaped Connie's lips as the wheels went over the brow of the hill, momentarily tipping the coach nearly to the point of going over onto its side. She wondered how Savannah was faring inside the narrow coffin?

"Here ya are, folks," the Sergeant huffed, as he led the team to the front of a tent much larger than the others. "If y'all don't mind gettin' down I'll take ya ta the Captain." Helping Connie then Ida from their perch, high on top of the dead-wagon, he turned to Ida. "I'm right sorry I ruffled your feathers back there ma'am. I didn't mean ta show no disrespect ta yer boys or nothin'. The Yankees are smugglin' all kinds 'a stuff back 'n forth across the border. We got orders ta search everythin' what comes this way. Shucks, I'm a fightin' soldier myself 'n I right admire them two young 'uns inside there. Any man what gives his life fer the Confederacy had ought ta be escorted ta the buryin' place, least ways the way I figure. Please don't think too unkind 'a me. I was just doin' what I was ordered ta do."

"That's okay young man. I'm sure you didn't mean any disrespect. It's only that I still can't accept the fact that my only sons lay inside those dreadful coffins," Ida sobbed, as she rubbed her eyes with the corner of her handkerchief and once more the tears flowed freely. "I still picture them as the day they enlisted. They stood by the door for me to admire them, so proud in those gray uniforms.

When you opened that coffin and the odor hit me, I realized that they were no longer the beautiful boys that I sent to war. I don't blame you in the least, Captain."

"Shucks ma'am, I ain't nothin' but a plain ol' ordinary Sergeant. The Captain, he's inside the tent there. If y'all could wait a minute I'll have Cobb fetch 'im. I'm sure it won't take too long 'n y'all can be on yer way again." Turning to the man who had opened the coffin he muttered something to him and Cobb disappeared inside the tent, only to reappear to hold the tent flap open for the officer.

By this time most of the soldiers had stopped their chores and surrounded the coach. Most were interested in the ornate craftsmanship around the glass windows, while more than a few ogled the pretty young woman dressed in black. Connie was very uncomfortable under the scrutiny and clung to Tom's arm. Beneath the heavy coat she could feel his arm tremble and this added to her discomfort. She patted his hand in an attempt to bolster his strength and received a weak smile for her efforts.

"What in the name of all that's holy is that thing doin' here?" A young officer approached the coach. As the crowd separated to let him through he saw Connie and Ida for the first time. "Sorry for my vile language ladies. I reckon I shouldn't be surprised at nothin' I see in this here war, but I sure didn't expect ta see one `a these."

"They was comin' down the road as pretty as ya please there Captain," the one called Cobb volunteered. "Got a right ripe corpse in that coffin atop the wagon, 'n another 'un inside. Checked that one on top myself, I did, 'n he's plumb bad."

"I believe that you've said quite enough Private," the officer interrupted. "If it's all the same to you I will hear the story from these folk's own lips. Now who are y'all, 'n what are ya doin' traipsin' around on that thing?"

"We are taking this woman's sons home for burial," Tom explained. "They were killed in a train derailment just outside of Atlanta. Seems the Yankees tore up the tracks and when the train hit there these two brothers were killed." Holding the top hat between his forefinger and thumb of both hands, Tom slowly rotated the brim in circles as he spoke. "I am the uncle of these boys and I also happen to be an undertaker. I have shown the papers to the Sergeant here and he believes everything is in order."

"I will decide what is and what is not in order here, sir. My name is Captain James Walsh and I am the commanding officer of this camp." His eyes shifted to the hat, which Tom held tightly against his stomach, as he continued to rotate the brim. "You seem unusually nervous, sir. Is there a particular problem that's bothering you?"

"Bothering me," Tom echoed, "of course there's something bothering me. This whole situation is bothering me. Our only sin is that we wish a decent burial for these boys, and here we are being detained by troops of the finest army in the country. They fought bravely for the same cause that you represent and we are treated as common highwaymen. Yes Captain, I would say that I have good cause to be bothered."

Losing none of his composure James waited for Tom to finish his tirade then he continued. "You are suspected of nothing. It's our duty to check every person, wagon, or anything else that passes down that road. If y'all have papers and they are in order, you will be free to go and not a moment before. Now if I can see your papers we won't hold you any longer than necessary."

"The papers are in a packet on the seat," Tom mumbled. "I'll get them for you, if that is if I'm allowed to."

"Please don't bother yourself, sir," the officer smiled at him. "Cobb, y'all climb up there 'n fetch me that packet."

Doing as he was ordered, the packet was soon in Captain Walsh's hands. As he opened the flap and removed the papers, Tom began to slide the hat brim between his fingers again. As one by one James examined the documents, the rest stood silent. The group of men that surrounded the coach and it's occupants, had now grown to the entire company.

"I take it that you are the mother and sister of the two boys?" James asked as he looked at Connie and Ida. The only response was a nod from each, as he thumbed through more of the papers. "And y'all are takin' them home ta Kentuck for burial, is that right?" Again he received a nod. "And you sir," he said as he held an envelope in his hands and read the address, "are Mister Thomas

Monroe Judd, is that right?"

"As it plainly states on the envelope, my name is Thomas Monroe Judd," Tom fairly shouted at the officer. "Can't anyone in this place read plain English?"

"Tom Judd, ya old skunk, I ain't seen ya in.....," a young corporal shoved his way through the crowd, followed by a youth wearing the insignia of drummer on his cap.

"Do ya know this man, Chet?" James asked as he looked at the soldier. "Can ya vouch for him?"

"Thomas Monroe Judd got his horse shod at Pa's shop 'n stayed at our house, 'bout five years 'fore I signed up. I know him well enough. I can vouch for Tom, but this fella ain't Thomas Monroe Judd. Never seen this fe...."

Before Chet could finish his sentence the hat fell from Tom's hands and the pepperbox pistol sent a bullet deep into Chet's chest. He slumped to the ground, his eyelids slightly fluttered and a barely audible expulsion of air from his lungs, was the final earthly thing that Chester Baxter did. The drummer threw himself on the dead soldier and sobbed. Tom took advantage of the shock that stunned everyone and attempted to break through the crowd. Overpowered by sheer numbers, he was disarmed and dragged back to the officer who was kneeling over the fallen soldier.

"Sergeant, tie his arms and tie 'em tight. The rest of you men tend to Chet 'n Tim there. Bring these three inta my tent 'n I want two guards outside. Sergeant, I want y'all ta stand right behind this fella, 'n if he even twitches ya got orders ta shoot him. Cobb, y'all take two men 'n open up them coffins 'n anything else they got in that coach."

"Sir," Cobb started to protest, "I done opened that one on top 'n take my word fer it, whatever's inside that there coffin is sure 'nuff dead. Sure don't hanker ta smell that again."

"Take the coach ta the far end 'a the camp 'n do as I tell ya. I want a detailed description of everythin' in them coffins." James's face grew red at the enlisted man's backtalk. "Ya can either do as I say, or spend the rest 'a the war inside a stockade in Chattanooga for insubordination. You three follow me and, for your own sakes, don't do nothin' stupid, like he's already done."

Once inside the tent, the flap was closed and the three were ordered to sit in chairs facing a table covered with maps and scraps of paper. A stern Captain Walsh stood before the entrance to the tent, his arms crossed and a grim look on his face. The Sergeant held a cocked pistol at Tom's back and, by placing one hand on his shoulder, held him into the chair.

"Now it's time ta get ta the bottom 'a this matter," James said solemnly. "Before I begin, I must tell you, Mister Tom Judd or whatever your name is, that you will be charged with the murder of a soldier of the Confederate States of America. By Chet's last words, y'all ain't what ya claim ta be. Exactly who and what are you? Don't make it any harder on yourself by lyin' ta me, for if ya do I'll have ya shot on the spot. Is that perfectly clear ta y'all?"

"My real name is Clayton Mc Nalley. As long as I'm going to hang for killing that young man, I may as well tell you the whole story. Before I begin though, please believe me. I am truly sorry for taking that boy's life. I panicked when he was about to give me away and I acted without realizing what I was doing."

"Why on earth did you deceive us into believing that you were Tom Judd?" A very confused and surprised Connie asked.

"By trade, I am a professional gambler. I was in a saloon in Truckee Meadows one evening when a fellow sat at the poker table. He was well dressed and seemed to be well heeled, wealthy to you ladies. He played well and won nearly every hand. After the game I engaged him in conversation and learned that his name was Thomas Judd. He showed me a letter from a plantation owner in Georgia asking him to come. He informed me that he had received word that the elderly gentleman was near death and that he was leaving in the morning. Traveling east he would catch a train at the first available stop. Because my luck had run badly that evening he offered to put me up with him at the hotel. We talked well into the night. The more I learned more about him, the more I envied him. By the time that we went to bed I had decided to accompany him. The next morning I sold everything I owned except my horse and tack and we left together. A plan began to formulate in my head. I would ask him of his private life, about his home, of Hamblin Garner, everything that I could think of. On the trail the time passes very slowly and he was more than happy to talk about his life. By the time we were nearing Salt Lake City, I knew more about Tho-

157

mas Judd than his own mother did."

A barrage of cat-calls and whistles coming from outside the tent stopped his talking. The tent flap flew open and Cobb hastily entered. "'scuse me sir, but I reckon y'all better see what me 'n the boys found in that there other coffin. Sure is anythin' but a corpse, or if it is I'll take a dozen just like it. Right nice lookin' body, ain't it sir?"

Connie looked in the direction in which Cobb was gawking. There stood Savannah, her hair in disarray, her face pale and her dress wrinkled, but still the lady. Her trembling hands held her skirt out of the dirt and her head held high. A soldier on each side held her by the arms as she was led into the tent.

"This gets more complicated by the minute. Do you have any more surprises for me, or can I continue?" James said as he wiped his brow. "If you please, bring another chair Mister Cobb." Soon Savannah was seated between Ida and Connie, while the one they had known as Tom Judd continued his story.

"Tom and I were just twenty miles or so out of Salt Lake when I decided that the time had arrived to carry out my plan. He had told me of a rather large bank account that Hamblin had set aside for him in Georgia, which made it all the more enticing. When we turned in for the night I waited until I could hear him breathing deeply in sleep. I planned to knock him out and tie him loose enough that he could free himself in a few hours. I would take the horses; leave a canteen of water and a saddlebag of food. This would last him until he could walk to Salt Lake. I figured that it would take him about four days to walk that distance and by then I'd be well out of the territory."

As he stopped and looked down at the dirt floor, the pause that followed made everyone sit a bit straighter. "What happened next, I really didn't mean to happen. I guess I hit him harder than I had intended to. Unintentionally I killed Tom Judd. There was nothing that I could do then except to carry out the rest of my plan, bury him and run. I took his clothes, his wallet and everything he had, even his name. From that day on I became Thomas Monroe Judd and was on my way to Cyprus Wood Plantation to be the over-seer."

"What would you have done if my grandfather had lived?"

Connie interrupted him. "Would you have killed him also?"

"No Connie, I would have never done that. All I had started out to be was a common thief, and I ended up killing a man by accident. The first thing I did, when I arrived in Rome, was to go the local cemetery and search for Hamblin Garner's grave. When I found none, I was about to move on. No one knew who I was, or what my business was. I had plenty of money from Tom's wallet. What was there would last me for a long time and I was about to leave Rome. In any town the best places to get information is either the local barber emporium or the local saloon. It didn't take me long in the barber's chair to learn that your grandfather had passed away, and that everyone was waiting to see what this Tom Judd looked like. Enter Clayton Mc Nalley, alias Tom Judd. Everyone welcomed me with open arms and I actually began to believe that I was who I pretended to be."

"If all that falter-all is true," Ida said bluntly, "when was it that you found Savannah in that overturned wagon? Seems to me that folks would wonder, or did you hide her in the bushes too?"

"That part I should leave up to Savannah to tell you. I shall neither confirm or deny what I have told you about her." Tom looked apologetically at Savannah. "It's entirely up to you my dear. You need not say anything, if you so wish."

"I believe that Connie has the right to know the truth," Savannah replied. Turning to Captain Walsh, she said softly. "This is a very private matter sir. Could you please give us a moment alone? I give you my word that there will be no attempt to escape."

James Walsh stroked his chin for a moment and then said sternly. "I will give you two a moment alone, however that man and the older lady will go outside with us. If you should attempt to escape, they will both be shot on the spot." Leading the way out of the tent James motioned for the rest to follow.

Waiting until she and Connie were alone and the tent flap dropped, Savannah took Connie's hand. "This is not an easy task, for me, and more than likely will be unbelievable to you. I know that you will have many questions, however please let me finish before you deluge me with them. The whole truth Connie is that you and I are related. Your grandmother had a black house servant by the name of Jennie. After your grandmother died, Master Ham and

Jennie fell in love and shortly after that I came along. It is not an uncommon practice in the south for plantation owners to have children by their slaves. Master Ham raised me as his own child. I was educated and dressed just like any white girl, however I was never allowed to leave Cyprus Wood. When he took sick he called me to his bedside and impressed upon me how important it was that you never learn the truth. When Master Tom arrived I told him the entire story and we concocted the tale you were told. We even coached Moses and Ceil as to what to say. You always felt a definite but unexplainable affinity towards me. Perhaps it's because we have the same blood running through our veins. That's the complete story and all I ask is that you don't hate me for the deception."

"Hate you," Connie replied. "Right now I'm too stunned to know exactly what my emotions are, however I definitely do not hate you. It's just that I am having a hard time adjusting to everything that has happened in the past few minutes."

"Your time's up, ladies," James Walsh said as he entered the tent, followed by Ida and the well-guarded Clayton McNalley.

"Could you please tell us what will happen to us now, Captain?" Connie asked after the tent flap was closed behind the Sergeant.

"I'm afraid that's beyond my control," he answered somberly. "I've sent a rider to the garrison at Chattanooga to bring back officers to hold a trial. It's out of my jurisdiction because I witnessed the murder of Chet Baxter. I could hardly be impartial so now someone else must preside. They should return in less than a week. Until that time the four of you will be under arrest. This is the largest tent in the camp, so you ladies will be bunked here. That man will be taken to the far end of the compound where he will be housed. I will warn y'all right now, there will be armed guards at each corner of your tents. Any attempt to escape and you will be immediately shot. Take the male prisoner to the tent next to the cooking tent." The man who had pretended to be Tom Judd gave Connie a look of helplessness. "I haven't given you many reasons to trust me in the past few hours, but please believe me now. I truly hold you in great regard and I'm sorry for what you are about to go through because of me." As he stepped toward Connie he was grasped by the Sergeant and quickly ushered out of the tent.

"Goodnight ladies," Captain Walsh said. With a gentlemanly bow he walked out of the tent, leaving the three women to ponder their fate.

CHAPTER TEN.

After the candle had been extinguished and total darkness settled over the tent a very confused Connie lay on her cot. The thought ran over and over in her head. "How could her grandfather be responsible for bringing a half-breed child into the world?" She remembered the closeness between him and her grandmother and found this too hard to believe. Doubt replaced confusion, and then reality replaced doubt. The pieces of the puzzle just didn't seem to fit as they should. How could she respect a man who had conceived a child with a slave woman?

"Savannah," she said softly, "tell me more about my grandfather and your mother. I want to know all about her. Where she came from and how she happened to end up at Cyprus Wood. I'm so confused at all that has happened, that I must know everything and try to sort this thing out. I'm sure that your mother was a very fine woman, however I just can't accept that my grandfather would, or could, be unfaithful to my grandmother."

"My mother was brought from Cuba. Since a child she had been trained to be the house servant of a rich owner of a sugar cane plantation. From what I have been told, your grandparents went to the slave auction. Master Ham had already bought a few slaves when Jennie was put on the block. Her skin was the color of coffee laced with generous amounts of fresh cream and a very beautiful woman. It was your grandmother who insisted that they had to have her, so Master Ham bought her. Before your grandmother passed away my mother was her constant companion at Cyprus Wood. For four years she was a personal servant to only the mistress. Upon her death Jennie became the personal servant of Master Ham, and three years or so later I came along. Master Ham was never unfaithful to your grandmother. Even after I was older, I still remember him going to her grave. He would sit there for hours talking to Mistress Anna, just as if she were standing beside him. He would tell her of the day's activities, or of particular problems that he was having. Every day he would have the grave cleared of any debris and fresh flowers would be placed there. I don't remember how old I was when he took me to the grave and introduced me to her. To a child that age it seemed more than strange. Why should she be formally introduced to a woman who had been dead these many years? When my mother died she was buried on the other side of the oak, away from your grandmother."

"If he loved you so much," Ida interrupted, "why didn't he free you? Somehow owning a slave that's your own flesh and blood seems mighty odd to me. You people certainly have strange customs, down south."

"Slaves must be registered in a book, much like the ones sea captains keep," Savannah answered, her voice wavering. "They record what the slave was named, who the parents were, what they are trained for and any other pertinent information. If the slave should go to the block, the better the records the higher price they bring. My birth was never registered anyplace. Not only was I a non-person in the south, I never existed anywhere. Please believe me Connie; I loved your grandfather as much as any child loves her father. Cyprus Wood was my entire world and Master Ham was my Lord. He did everything that any father would do for his child, except give me his name. He was the kindest and most gentle person that I have ever seen and he spoke often of you."

"When this fellow came posing as Tom Judd, Ham was already dead then?" Ida interrupted again. "So when this stranger appeared, he moved in and took Ham's place as master of the plantation. Did he take over ownership of you too?"

"First of all, no one took Master Ham's place in the hearts of anyone at the plantation. All Master Tom was to me was a confidant and nothing more. There was closeness between us because we shared a secret that no one else knew, except for Ceil and Moses. We only shared a secret and nothing more. I was as surprised by what happened today as either of you, if not more so. Master Ham talked often of this Tom Judd and how they had met. He even described him numerous times. When the man arrived, claiming to be Tom Judd, he fit the description and had all the papers, so no questions were asked. There is nothing left to tell, unless there is something that you would like to ask?"

"I believe that you have answered most of what has been bothering me," Connie said hesitantly. "I must try to sort all of this out, perhaps then I will have more to ask." With that the three women grew silent, each with their own thoughts running through their heads.

Dawn was just breaking when a drum roll awakened them. Covering their shoulders with a blanket against the chill of the morning air, the women dressed and awaited the next portion of this day. Each sat on their cot, watching the flicker of the candle play patterns on the walls of the tent.

"Are y'all decent?" The Sergeant's voice called from outside the flap. "If ya are, the Captain wants y'all ta come 'n get some grub 'fore the rest 'a the troops eat. He don't think it's a good idea fer ya ladies ta sashay 'round in front 'a the men. Might take their minds off what they's here fer," he added with a chuckle.

"Grub," consisted of a pasty helping of porridge and a cup of chicory, neither of which was really palatable. Ordered to stay in their tents until the women left the compound didn't stop the soldiers from leering at them. The flap of every tent was open enough for eyes to be seen watching their every movement. As they passed one tent a snide remark was made at Ida, who stopped in her tracks and directed her answer to the unseen man inside.

"Mister, if I look good to you, you have been on the lines much too long. I suggest that you ask to be sent home for the duration of this war," sarcasm laced her voice. "I have no idea of what you look like, however I am certain that I wouldn't be seen with you at a dog fight."

Confined to the tent for the rest of the day the women passed the time in small talk. A plate of beans was brought to them for lunch. Later they were informed that after dark they would be allowed into the compound for a brief walk. Until then they were to stay inside and not complicate matters by even opening the flap on the tent.

So went the next few days. The monotonous routine began to bother them, however there was nothing that they could do until the officers arrived to hold court. The lad, who was the drummer, started to bring their food and would attend to their needs. They learned his name was Timothy Baxter, from Hannibal, Missouri and that the soldier that had been killed was his only surviving family member. They never had so much as a glimpse of the man who had passed himself off as Tom. Whenever they were allowed out of their tent, the flap of his tent was closed tightly shut.

It was just after the drummer had sounded the roll for lights out when a shout, followed by two shots, made them jump. Rushing to the tent flap they peered out into the compound. By the light of the many torches they saw the man named Clayton Mc Nalley, dressed only in his under bottoms, sprawled face down on the ground. They watched in silence as the body was dragged away and the turmoil subsided. There was to be no sleep for the women that night. Each lay on their beds thinking of how they had been fooled by that man and he would fool no one ever again.

They were not allowed to leave the tent for breakfast the next morning. Instead the drummer boy brought their plates to them. " What happened out there last night Tim?" Connie asked. "We heard the shots and saw them drag the body away, but we were too far away to catch any of the details."

"T'ain't much ta tell ma'am. That fella what shot Chet just tried ta run 'n them soldiers shot 'im dead. Heard tell that there was a big timber rattler coiled under the blanket in his bed, 'n when he climbed in he got bit 'n bit good. Reckon he just went plumb crazy 'n tried ta run from that there snake 'n got shot for his efforts. They's lots 'a them rattlers 'round here, so's a person's got ta be right careful where he puts his legs."

"How in the world would a snake climb into a persons bed?" Ida asked. "These cots are a good two feet off the floor. It would take a mighty long snake to climb that high."

"Snakes are just like us people," the boy answered. "They like ta be warm 'n comfortable too. It's not nothin' ta find one inside a person's boot, or anyplace warm 'n cozy. Shucks, I done seen a snake climb right up a tree 'n eat the eggs out 'a the birds nest.

They can go 'bout anywhere's they got a mind ta. I seen them timber rattlers as long as five foot." Waiting for the women to eat what little of the breakfast that they wanted, Tim took the dishes and left the tent.

It was late that afternoon when the three officers arrived at the camp. After a briefing by James Walsh the trial was set for ten o'clock the next morning. Because the prime reason for the trial was already deceased, it promised to be relatively short. A long rough-hewn table was set in the center of the compound, while the company flag and the Confederate Battle Flag were placed at either end. Chairs were set behind the table and three more in front. All was in readiness for tomorrow and the future of the three women would be decided for them.

When Tim brought them breakfast the morning of the trial, they fervently hoped that this was not an omen of what was to come. Instead of the usual mush a heaping plate of ham and fried eggs were doled out to each woman. Was this offering to be the condemned person's last meal? At the appointed hour four guards escorted Ida, Connie and Savannah to the center of the compound, where the officers were already seated behind the table. Ushered to their respective chairs they were ordered to sit and the trial began.

"This court is now in session," a man wearing the insignia of Colonel on his lapel announced loudly. "We have convened this hearing to try a man for murder and you three ladies as accomplices to that crime. Because the main defendant is already dead, it narrows it down to only your guilt or innocence. Captain Walsh has thoroughly briefed us about the incident concerning the murder of a soldier of the Confederacy. I must tell y'all, that if any or all of you are found guilty of conspiracy, you will be hanged. We want the truth of your relationship to the man that killed Corporal Baxter. We need any other pertinent information you may give to help us reach a conclusion."

The voice droned on, however none of the three heard much as the threat of being hung repeated over and over in their heads. This couldn't really be happening. Conspiracies to commit what crime were they being accused of?

"Which of you is Miss Constance Garner?" The voice echoed

in her ears before Connie stood up. "I see by the will enclosed in this packet, that you are from Martindale, Pennsylvania, is that correct?" Too numb to answer verbally, Connie simply nodded. "You were left the plantation of Hamblin Garner, is that also correct?" Another nod and he continued. "Tell this court how you came to be traveling in the company of the accused man, and your attempted to hide run away Negro slave."

Finding her voice Connie told of the arrival at Cyprus Wood, of meeting the man passing himself off as Tom Judd and how the war was coming ever closer to Georgia. "The only thoughts that any of us had was to get to freedom as soon as possible. There was no train travel so Tom came up with this idea. We are guilty of nothing except wanting to get back home and away from the fighting. There is no run away slave among us. Ida is my trusted housekeeper and has been since before my parents died. Savannah is my aunt. She lived at Cyprus Wood and was as much in danger as the rest of us, so naturally we were taking her north with us."

"If that's the case, why were y'all sneaking her out inside a coffin?" The Colonel's demeanor grew sterner. "Are ya aware that it's a capitol offence to help a slave escape? Y'all may be from north of the line, however when you are in the south our laws, not the ones from Philadelphia, restrict you. This woman is obviously black and from all outward appearances, y'all were attempting to sneak her out of the south."

"She was hidden for the very reason that you are assuming now," Connie snapped back defiantly. "After my grandmother died grandfather married a woman of Indian blood, Seneca I believe. Savannah can't help her skin color any more than you or I can, but we knew that someone would mistake her for colored. Our biggest fear was that the slave runners would find her and she would be hung before we could explain. That is the reason she was hidden in the coffin and none other. Even if she were black, since when is it a crime to be a person of color?"

"There is no crime at all, young lady and I'd suggest that you show this court a little more respect. At this period in time it hardly seems that any of y'all are in a position to be haughty. I suggest that you read the Dread Scott Decision, passed by your own congress. In there it clearly states that, 'Slaves are property and not citizens of the United States'. It also basically says, 'That slaves have no rights under the constitution.' Can you prove that she is of Indian ancestry and not black?'"

"This nonsense has gone far enough," Ida blurted out as she jumped to her feet. "Can you prove that your forefathers are of Irish, or German, or whatever? Do you think that because Savannah came from a tribe that most whites consider inferior, she should carry a certificate stating her origin around with her? You sir, are assuming too much and presuming her guilt before she is tried. In the north a person is presumed innocent until their guilt is proven. I naturally assumed that it was the same in the south, or is my assumption wrong?"

"Your assumption is quite correct," the Colonel's attitude seemed to soften a bit. "None of us, seated at this table are attorneys. As such we are not blessed with legal minds, so we must determine the guilt or innocence by using common sense and the evidence provided to us. As of now the only one of you that can show us any evidence of who they are, is Miss Garner. We have her word that you are her housekeeper and that lady is her aunt and nothing more. There is nothing in any of these papers to substantiate either of those statements. It is my opinion that if this were a simple case of trying to hide a slave, it would be open and shut. You would be free to go on your way, however this involves the murder of a soldier and that complicates matters. With the aid of Captain Walsh, we three have spent most of the night going over these papers one by one. If, as you say that Savannah is really the child of Hamblin Garner and an Indian woman, why was no mention of her made in the will, or any of the rest of these papers?"

A stunned silence fell on the three women then Ida stood again. "I don't know what's in those papers, but are you going to convict a girl simply because her name doesn't appear on any of them? There are trunks of papers that we had to leave behind at Cyprus Wood. Because of the cramped conditions we were allowed to only bring the absolute necessities. I was informed by the housekeeper at Cyprus Wood that the reason that Connie was left the plantation, was because Savannah had chosen to rejoin her people. She went alone to rejoin her mother's tribe. Rejected by her people for being part white she returned to the plantation, Ham was already dead when she arrived." It was a bald faced lie and Ida hoped that it didn't show on her face.

The officers held a quiet conversation before the Colonel spoke again. "We are willing to give y'all the benefit of the doubt. This court will adjourn for two hours so we can go over the papers again and deliberate a verdict. Is there anything else y'all want to say before we adjourn?" There was only silence from the women. "This court stands adjourned for two hours. Sergeant, return the prisoners to their tents until we summon them again."

Without a doubt the time spent waiting was the longest of any of their lives. Ida fidgeted on the edge of her cot, while Connie paced the confines of the tent and Savannah held her face in her hands. Expecting the Sergeant when the flap opened they jumped to their feet, however it was Tim who entered.

"Thought maybe, y'all'd like a cup 'a tea. T'ain't real tea, but leaves from a brush that Ma used ta drink all the time. It's a might bitter, so I poured a spoon 'a molasses in it. Watch them tin cups though, they gets mighty hot." Handing each lady a cup he sat on the edge of the cot. "I don't reckon y'all's got much ta fret yourselves over. If I was the judge, I'd let y'all off 'n send ya on yer way. T'waren't none 'a y'all what shot Chet, 'n the fella what done it's dead too. I jus' hope them judges believe that there story 'bout Savannah. The whole thing swings on that."

"What will you do now, Tim?" Connie asked between sips of the brew. "With no one to look after you and the last of your family gone, will they let you stay in the army?"

"Shucks ma'am," he answered, "I ain't in no army. They just let me play soldier 'n bang on that there drum, but if it come ta a shootin' war they'd ship my tail out ta here quick. Don't know what I'm gonna do now Chet's gone. T'ain't nothin' left back home 'n I reckon I got just 'nuff 'a Pa's wanderlust ta want ta know what's over the next hill. Pa always wanted ta head west 'n never made it, maybe I'll do it fer 'im. Who knows, I just might strike it rich somewhere's. Heard they's lots a silver back in that new territory 'a Nevada. Might just get me some 'a that 'n live it up in that place 'a San Francisco. Ya hear 'bout lots 'a places from the different soldiers."

The tent flap opened and the Sergeant stuck in his head. "The courts all ready ta start again ladies. The Colonel sent me ta fetch y'all back ta the table." Walking a few steps behind him they did as they were bid and sat in the chairs again.

"This court is again in session," the Colonel said as he cleared his throat. "We have gone over every scrap of evidence and have reached a verdict. Is there anything any of y'all want ta say before the verdict is read?"

"For heaven sakes, get on with it," Ida said, more to herself than anyone else. Receiving a scowl from the Colonel, she shrunk back into her chair. "Sorry sir," she mumbled an apology.

"Since Mrs. Cramer is in such an all fired hurry ta get this over with, it is the verdict of this court that there is no evidence linking any of you to the murder of Corporal Baxter, or any other crime for which you should be tried. Whether Savannah is of Negro or Indian blood is not considered a military matter at this time. We apologize to each of you for the inconvenience and you are free to go. Here is your packet back, and a letter allowing you to pass through our lines without any further delays. It also requests that the Union army extend the same courtesy to y'all as ya travel through Yankee territory. It explains the trial, the decision and the reasons for y'all traveling alone. This court is adjourned."

The three women jumped to their feet and embraced each other. The three officers came around the table and congratulated each of them and received profuse thanks for the verdict. The Colonel approached Ida and laid a hand on her arm.

"If y'all ever get tired 'a bein' a housekeeper, I think your niche would be better suited to law. I'd hate ta be some trial lawyer facin' an opponent with your disposition. Y'all will be free ta leave anytime that suits ya and God's speed. Goodbye ladies." Turning on his heels he led the other officers to their tent.

"Though you're no longer technically under arrest, If you ladies don't mind, I still got a whole camp ta run," James Walsh said as he approached the three women, with Tim on his heels. " I must ask ya to return ta your tent, 'cause I won't get nothin' out 'a these men long as you're in sight. I have a wagon at your disposal 'n I'm havin' a spare seat put in it. We're keepin' the coach 'n one team 'a horses. I hope y'all don't mind, but the south's kind's shy on horseflesh 'n that dead wagon'd draw too much attention ta y'all.

Tim here's gonna take y'all as far as the closest railhead, then y'all can get on a train for home 'n then he's on his own. Seems like he's had all the army life he wants, 'n I don't want nothin' ta happen ta him. Let me know when y'all want ta leave 'n everythin'll be ready for ya."

"If tomorrow isn't too soon, we'd like to leave in the morning," Connie said, happy at the prospects of seeing Martindale as soon as possible, "and thank you for your many kindness' Captain Walsh."

"Tomorrow morning it will be," he replied as he returned her smile. "If y'all can have everythin' ready to load, I'll have it packed away for ya 'n y'all can be on your way. I hope y'all have a pleasant journey 'n that the worst is behind ya. Tim may be small, but he's a real soldier 'n he'll look after ya real good. Now if y'all will follow me, we can get ya back out 'a sight 'n I can get these men back ta work."

Somehow the tent didn't feel near as confining with the prospect of freedom facing them. Tim became a constant companion, nearly to the point of becoming a pest. He brought them cup after cup of the terrible tea, until they begged him to bring no more. When it was time for bed the women were exhausted, both mentally and physically. The lack of sleep the night before and the uncertainty of the trial had left them drained. They were all fast asleep long before the drum roll for lights out sounded. Even the excitement of going home failed to impede their slumber.

Hardly had the morning candle been lit and the women dressed before Tim was again waiting at the tent. A light mist was falling as Connie undid the flap and let him in. The uniform had been replaced with the patched coveralls and faded red shirt of a farm boy. His uncombed hair resembled a straw pile in a windstorm and a pair of shoes hung from the laces around his neck.

"Got the team all hitched 'n ready ta go," he proudly announced. "I figured y'all'd be rearin' ta go soon as it broke light. Got us a sack 'a food 'n Pa's scattergun fer company." The infectious grin spread across his freckled face as he joined Savannah sitting on the cot. "Rainin' a bit, so I got us slickers ta keep us dry on the road. Don't imagine y'all want ta wait 'round 'n eat no more 'a that army cookin', so's I tol' James we'd be leavin' at first light. Got a whoppin' way ta go, we do, 'n the sooner we start the sooner we get there."

"You did just fine Tim. There is one other thing you could do for us. There was a small box placed in the foot of the coffin that Savannah was hidden in. It appears that everyone was so busy with her that they stopped looking once she was found. Inside that box is everything that I have left of Cyprus Wood Plantation. I would appreciate it if you could find a way to put it in the wagon without anyone seeing you do it. Now if you'll leave us alone we will get our things together and meet you at the wagon. Thank you for your thoughtfulness," Connie added as she held the flap open as an invitation to Tim to leave.

"That young man should have been born a girl," Ida muttered after he left. "I haven't seen a person that anxious since my late husband found the corner saloon. Okay ladies, let's get packed or he will be back in two minutes wondering what's keeping us."

The rain had stopped when James Walsh and the Sergeant met them at the wagon. After numerous good-byes and expressions of thanks, Tim took the reins and slapped them against the flanks of the team. Jerking into motion the wagon turned back toward the main road, somewhere at the end of which was home.

Topping the rim and turning north, the faint glimmer of remorse touched Tim. Turning for one final glance behind, he snapped the horses into a ground-eating trot. "So long Chet," he said to himself. "Hope the fishin's real good where ya are now 'n I'm sure gonna miss ya. I sure am. Save a couple fer me 'n maybe someday we can drown a worm together again. I reckon I really am the man of the family now, ain't got no choice, seein' as how I am the family. Say 'Hi,' ta Pa, Ma 'n the twins fer me. I'm gonna make it Chet. I really am gonna make it on my own. Bye.'"

"Are you alright Tim?" Ida's voice had a tone of sympathy that was seldom shown. "We know it's hard for you to leave all your friends behind. Once we get back to Martindale I'll bake you the biggest and best apple pie that you have ever tasted." Attempting to get his mind from what he was leaving behind to something more cheerful, Ida continued. "We'll take you and Savannah to Philadelphia. I'll bet you have never seen a place as big as that. There must be nearly nine or ten thousand people living there."

"Always been a country boy," Tim responded. "Never hankered to see no big cities. Tell the truth they'd scare the manure out 'a me. Saw St. Louis one time. Got lost 'n never want ta do that again. I really thought I'd die for sure 'fore the folks found me. Thanks for the offer, but I don't know exactly what I'm gonna do. We still got a long way ta go 'fore we're out 'a this mess. Who knows, maybe even Martindale could look good ta me by then." Lapsing into silence once again, he slapped the reins on the horse's rumps and settled back into the seat; pleasant thoughts of the past filled his mind. He envisioned the concentric rings forming when he and his brothers tossed pebbles into the pond. Of skipping rocks across the water and counting to see who had the most before the rock sank beneath the surface. Small things, like tying the legs of the twins pants into knots and pulling them so tight they had a difficult time undoing his handiwork. Of frog gigging by torchlight and the smell of frog legs frying in Ma's big skillet. These memories of the past were all he had left and he savored each of them. What lie ahead was an unknown future.

CHAPTER ELEVEN.

The days seemed as never ending as the winding road ahead. Though it had been but twelve days since leaving the army camp behind, it seemed an eternity. The uncertainty of what lies at the end of this journey, or even around the next bend, had been wearing on everyone. An occasional sharp word, followed by a hasty apology, was the only indication of the stress everyone felt. Tim sat alone in the driver's seat, while the three ladies attempted to keep from breathing the infernal dust kicked up by the horses. Hunkering behind the seat they raised their knees and buried their faces in the folds of their dresses. Tying his handkerchief over his nose and mouth helped filter some of it out, but the grit still found its way through the fabric and into the very spaces between his teeth. Dipping his head he squinted to keep it from filling his eyes also, but to little avail. The dirt road seemed to meander on forever, disappearing around one bend only to reappear as an endless ribbon further on. It was a never changing country of thickets so heavy that visibility was barely twenty feet on either side. Tim only hoped that if it hid troops, be they Yankee or Rebel, that they would challenge them first rather than start shooting.

"Are you alright Tim?" Connie's voice made him turn in the seat and look into the back of the wagon. "Would you mind stopping for a while. I believe we all need some water to wash this Tennessee dirt out of our throats."

Lifting the bottom of the handkerchief Tim managed to mumble in the affirmative, before the dust choked him with the next breath.

He was more than ready to climb down from the seat and breathe fresh air again. The once sleek black horses were now a dull white-gray where the sweat mixed with the dust and caked. Straining his eyes against the grit Tim searched for a spot large enough to pull the team off the trail. The vegetation covering the roadside seemed impenetrable and grew thicker as they went. It was nearly an hour before he managed to locate a narrow trail, barely wide enough to allow the wagon to maneuver on. In many places overhanging branches blotted out the sky, while clumps of Spanish moss hung from some of the limbs. Searching both sides Tim scanned the area for some signs of water but found none. Less than a half-mile off the main road the trail narrowed, then pinched off to a game trail.

"Looks like this is as far as we go on this road ladies," Tim said as he pulled the handkerchief from his face and jumped to the ground. "I only hope that there's enough room to turn this thing around down here. Somehow I just can't see me backin' up the horses all the way back to the road. I'm gonna unhitch 'em 'n give 'em a breather. They ate as much dust as we have 'n it most likely don't taste good to them neither. If one 'a y'all could hand me that there frypan, I'll water 'em just a bit." Dropping the traces he tied a rope around the neck of each animal before offering them water. "Soon as we find a stream wide enough ta fit ya, we'll wash the dirt off. Seems a real shame that animals as proud as y'all are has ta look like some ordinary work plug." Wetting his handkerchief he carefully wiped the dirt from away from the eyes and nostrils of both horses.

"You seem to have a way with animals," Savannah startled Tim as she had walked behind him unnoticed. "I admire anyone who treats any animal with kindness. Some consider those of my race on a par with a dog or horse. Perhaps that's why I empathize with any creature that is being treated badly."

Tim studied the fine olive features. To his point of view they were flawless. The large brown eyes, rimmed by the heavy lashes, and full lips were the only indication of possibly some colored blood. By the same token, Tim had seen the same features in a Creole woman back at Hannibal. A body never could say one way or the other that Savannah was definitely black. "I been around animals all my life," Tim responded, as he shifted his gaze from the beautiful face to where he was scuffing the dirt with the toe of his shoe. "Back home I had all kinds 'a wild critters for pets. Some Ma wasn't too fond of, like the baby coon I brought home. He liked ta sleep in the folk's bed. More 'n once they'd climb inta bed 'n get nipped when they disturbed the little critter. Pa finally made me take him back out ta the woods 'n turn him lose. Never saw him again, after that day."

"While we are on the subject of animals crawling into people's beds, there are still a few things that bother me about that snake in Tom's bed." Ida joined the conversation as she and Connie moved next to Savannah. "I didn't want to bring them up while we were still in that camp. I feared that the questions may keep us there longer while they searched for a solution." Ida now stood over Tim, her penetrating gaze seemed to drill into his very soul. He could almost hear his mother ask, "How was school today, boys," all the while knowing full well that they hadn't set foot inside the schoolhouse all day. He felt trapped now as he had felt then. Not daring to lie, yet not ready for the penalty for telling the truth.

"Don't reckon I know anythin' 'bout that ma'am," he busied himself with the team, in an attempt to keep from being drawn deeper into the subject before facing Ida again. "Them rattlers are strange critters. Likely ta find 'em most anywhere. 'specially warm places on cool nights. At different times back home we found a few behind our kitchen stove. Even had ta watch when we gathered eggs, 'cause sometimes they'd be a snake coiled inside the hen's nest. Yes sir, right unpredictable critters them rattlers are. Likely ta find 'em most anywheres."

"Perhaps," Ida continued to stare deep into Tim's eyes, "it was as you say and simply a reptile looking for a warm place to sleep, and then again, perhaps not. That evening was anything but cool and the tent where Tom was held was in the center of six other tents. How do you suppose that a snake would crawl unseen through a camp full of soldiers, past at least four other tents it could sleep in, and find it's way into the cot of a man who has four armed guards outside. Once past all of this, the brilliant reptile climbs the two-foot leg of the bed, slides under the neatly tucked blanket, then instead of settling in the first warm spot he comes to, crawls the entire length of the bed and settles in the foot where the covers are completely tucked in. It's almost as if someone deliberately put that snake in his bed. I'm not accusing anyone mind you. Heaven knows that he had everything coming to him and then some. It just seems that in this case, one and one makes three. The facts don't seem to justify the verdict. What do you think Tim?"

"I can't say one way or the other. I seen snakes climb trees 'n take birds right out 'a the nest, so I know for a fact that they can climb. Far as how it got that far inta camp without no one seein' it, I can't rightly say neither. Ya make sense questionin' 'bout how it got clear in the bottom 'a that bed. I wouldn't even make a guess on how it done that. Right mystifyin', it is. I reckon only the good Lord 'n that snake knows for a fact how it got there, 'n neither one 'a 'em's sayin' much." Turning his back on the women Tim tended the horses again, however Ida was not about to let the subject drop.

"You're knowledgeable on these things Tim. If you had to make a judgment call, would you personally say that someone apparently put the snake there on purpose?" Placing her hand on Tim's back she felt him stiffen at her touch.

"Shucks ma'am, I ain't nothin' but some country hick 'n nobody'd ever ask someone like me to make no call like that. First off, I can't guess no better 'n y'all the why's 'n how's of it all, 'n second, I don't see where it makes no difference nohow. Can't say I'm sorry he got snakebit 'n then shot, 'cause he's the one what shot Chet. I ain't gonna lose no sleep over the whole matter, no more 'n I'd cry over the snake what bit 'im. Reckon that it was just a case 'a one snake killin' another." Turning to face Ida, Tim brushed the hint of a tear from his eyes, leaving a moist ring in the dust collected on his face. "I don't know what ya want out 'a me Miss Ida, but if y'all want me ta say I put that snake in his bed 'n it'll end the subject, then I done it. I sneaked inta his tent in broad daylight, carryin' a big timber rattler past them four guards, tore his bed apart, put the snake in 'n made it up again without getting' bit myself. Yes ma'am, I done it just that way. Now, is that what y'all wanted ta hear? 'cause if it was, I got chores ta do 'fore we get on the trail again. I reckon y'all need ta clean up a bit too."

"Ida," snapped a very upset Connie, "I don't know what it is that you are trying to prove, but whatever it is you have carried it much too far. Tim can only guess what happened, the same as we.

He grew up in this wilderness and knows much more about the habits of reptiles than we do. If he thinks what happened is possible, then we have no reason to question him."

"I'm sorry Tim, I wasn't blaming you for anything. In spite of all that Tom, or whatever his name was, did, he still risked everything to help us to get back to Pennsylvania. If it weren't for us Tim's brother would still be alive, as would that imposter and none of this sorry mess would have happened." Placing an arm around Tim's shoulder Ida face softened. "In spite of the fact that he was a scoundrel, we still owe him a great debt and possibly our lives. Savannah might now be hanging from one of those trees lining the main road, while Connie and I decorated the other side for abetting an escaped slave."

"I hardly call a man who has killed two innocent men a scoundrel," Connie interrupted. "True, we do owe him a great debt, however he is not here to collect. He was a conniving thief, murderer, liar and con artist. I would say that his bad points far outweigh what pittance we may owe to that man. I believe the thing that bothers me the most is the fact that I believed every word he uttered. Worse than that, I believe that I was beginning to have some feelings for him that were more than sisterly."

"If he was smooth enough to fool an entire town, everyone at the plantation and all the neighbors for miles around, then why do you think that you should be any different? I have known him far longer than either you or Ida have, and I nurtured a great admiration for him. Many nights I would lie in my bed and wonder what my life would have been if I was completely white. Being a nonperson I knew that, as much as I wished, there would never be a chance for me to be anything but a servant to him." Savannah paused long enough to brush away some dust from her face with a handkerchief, then continued. "You can never know what it is like to never have any identity what-so-ever. Master Tom was the first white person, outside of my own father of course, to treat me like a real human being. I too wonder about the circumstances surrounding his death, but what is done is done and all the questions in the world will reverse nothing. I believe that we all owe Tim a debt of gratitude for all he is doing for us. Not many young men would care to be burdened with three women in the middle of a field of war."

Tim beamed at the praise that was being heaped upon him. "Shucks Miss Savannah, I ain't doin' nothin' special. I ain't got no where else ta go 'n all the time in the world ta get there. I right like the company of such pretty ladies. T'ain't often a fella gets the chance ta traipse about with such high caliber folks like y'all. 'sides, life sure been anythin' but dull since I met up with y'all. I got some tales ta tell my children, when I get older 'n have children that is. I won't even have ta stretch the truth none ta make it sound like a whopper. As much as I hate ta do it, I reckon we best be gettin' back on the way again, if y'all want ta get home 'fore the war ends that is." Turning his attention to the team he soon had them hitched to the wagon again. Pulling the bandanna over his face he climbed into the seat, while the women got into the back.

"Lead on mister liveryman," Ida's muffled voice came through the folds of her skirt, as she buried her face against the coming on slot of dust.

"T'ain't nobody here by that name, just got Timothy B. Baxter's in this seat," he said as he turned the horses for the main road again and clicked his tongue to get them moving. They had barely gone fifty yards when Tim pulled them to a halt and jumped from the seat.

"What in the world?" Ida asked, as she and the other women raised their heads and looked around. "Is there something the matter, Tim? Why are we stopped?"

"Nothin' the matter," he answered, "bout forgot somethin' I thought might belong ta ya ladies. We got caught up in talkin' 'bout the guy what killed Chet, 'n I forgot all about it. While y'all was at that trial, I got lookin' over that big wagon y'all come in. I looked at that coffin 'n decided ta climb in, just ta try it on for size, ya know, just for fun. I was layin' in that thing, when my foot hit somethin' that sounded a might funny, so I started lookin' around." Lifting a pile of blankets directly under the seat he exposed a familiar wooden box. "Reckon them soldiers was so excited ta find Miss Savannah, that they didn't look no further. I pulled it out 'n hid it in the bushes 'til we got ready ta leave, then hauled it here. I reckon it's the one ya asked me 'bout. I didn't open it, but that thing's sure heavy 'nuff."

"Timothy Baxter, I could kiss you," a jubilant Connie exclaimed as she studied the box. "You may have salvaged what little hope I had for something good to come from all this. This is indeed the box I asked you to get for me. Inside this little box is the total sum of my involvement at Cyprus Wood Plantation. Except for Savannah, everything else is but a memory and many unanswered questions."

"Mighty little box ta hold all that," Tim said as he brushed his hair away from his face. "Maybe we best put it back 'n get on our way again though. At this rate we won't never get y'all ta Philadelphia. We still got a mite 'a travelin' 'fore we can get y'all on a train north." Pushing the box beneath the blankets, Tim pulled himself back on top of the wagon seat and picked up the reins. Glancing over his shoulder he was certain the women were all safely aboard before moving the horses into a steady, but not strenuous ground eating, gait. Pulling the handkerchief over his face he again lowered his head against the dust. To pass the time away he attempted to sing, however the dust choked his words off short and he gave up. Now he simply ran the words and tunes through his mind, over and over again. He was in the midst of one such medley when the horses suddenly shied, jerking the wagon to one side. Two men in Union uniforms suddenly jumped from the covering at the roadside and grabbed the reins of the horses.

"Hold up, there," another yelled from the trees. "We got a dozen rifles aimed right at yer skinny body, so hold them hands right where they are. Jason, you get back 'n check the back 'a that wagon while Tony holds them nags still."

The shorter of the two left the team and sauntered lazily toward the wagon. Stepping on the spokes of the wheel he pulled himself up to peer over the side, only to be met with a resounding hit over the head by Ida's umbrella. He presented an almost comical sight as he fell backwards and tried to pull the revolver from the holster, break the fall with his other hand, and yell for help at the same time. Rolling in the dust he quickly regained his feet and, with pistol in hand, approached the wagon from the back this time. Two others had emerged from the foliage and were a few steps behind Jason. Two more had pulled Tim from the seat and held him fast against the rough boards of the side.

"What in the name of Nellie do we have here?" Jason exclaimed, as he was met by the sight of the three women huddled tightly against the back of the seat. "Luke, I reckon you'd best take a look at what that there squirt's got in the back of his wagon. Best lookin' freight I seen in many a moon. Wouldn't mind haulin' that myself."

"Unless you want another whack on that thick skull of yours," Ida stood up defiantly, "you had better keep a civil tongue. You even lay so much as a finger on either of these ladies and I will break you like a matchstick."

"Y'all best pay her some heed," Tim nodded his head. "That 'un's 'bout the roughest female I ever done met. Saw her personally take on a Reb Colonel 'n rip him right down ta a mere shadow 'a what he once was. She had him hollerin', 'Uncle,' 'for he even knew what was happenin'. I personally heard him tell her that she was rougher 'en any Yankee he ever seen.'"

"I'm Lieutenant Luke Hill. Just where did you have any meetin's with a Reb Colonel?" A voice from the opposite side of the wagon, made everyone turn in that direction. "We have been in these parts for over a month and have seen probably three dozen travelers, counting yourselves. This is not a well-traveled road, so anyone on it had best have a good reason for not being on the main thoroughfares and for taking a back road. If you have any travel papers I suggest that you produce them, and remember the guns aimed at all of you."

"Our papers are in our travel trunk, sir," Connie tried to be as amiable as possible under the circumstances. "It is that brown one at the far end of the wagon. All of the papers are lying on the very top and I'm certain that you will find everything in order. We are on our way to the nearest rail station that will allow us passage back to Philadelphia. By the looks of your uniforms we have at last reached the friendly north and a most welcome sight it is."

"Don't just stand there Jason, help the ladies down and then get those papers for me," the lieutenant ordered. "If all of you will be so kind as to follow us we will try to detain you for only a short while." His smile and smooth manner set them at ease and, gathering their skirts out of the dirt, the three women did as they were bid.

Tim was not as willing to follow. Something just didn't ring true. Perhaps it was because they were the hated Blue Bellies, or perhaps he was being overly cautious. Whatever the reason, he held back until someone behind him gave him a sharp jab in the back, with the muzzle of a rifle.

"Move on there Sonny. We ain't got no time for dallying." The gruff voice accentuated the jab. "What ya carryin' in that wagon that makes ya take the back roads? Must be somethin' ya want ta hide. Maybe I best have a look-see after the lieutenant gets finished with ya. Hey Luke, where ya want this one?" The lieutenant simply pointed and opened the envelope.

Moving closer to where the others had stopped, Tim stood on the fringes as the officer read the papers from the trunk. "How is it that you have a pass that's supposed to get you through our lines signed by some Reb? Takes a lot of gall for some Jonnie Reb to ask General Grants boys to obey his orders and let every Reb spy through our lines. Just can't see us doin' that little thing." Handing the papers back to Connie he turned to two soldiers at his elbow.

"Doc, you take Jason and search that wagon, the rest of you get back to where you are supposed to be."

"Doc," Tim half shouted. "Are y'all a regular doctor? Our prayers are answered ladies." Everyone stopped at the outburst and all eyes were on Tim. The women were as puzzled as any of the soldiers. "Doctor, ya got ta help Miss Savannah there. Don't rightly know what's wrong with her. We buried her sister just two days ago. She was awful sick 'n the doctor at that Rebel camp wouldn't tell us nothin'. He just examined her 'n the next thing we know, they put us on that there wagon 'n told us they'd shoot us if we come back. She had some kind 'a white spots in her mouth 'n funny red splotches on her body. The Reb doc said somethin' 'bout somethin' called, 'Fox,' what ever that is? Now Miss Savannah is startin' ta get the spots under her arms 'n them white spots inside her mouth.'"

"Are you certain that it wasn't Pox and not Fox, that he called it?" A look of concern crossed the faces of those close and they drew away from the women. "Think boy. Was it Pox?" The doctor's voice became agitated and he shook Tim by one arm.

"Might 'a been Pox," Tim slowly replied. "He was talkin' ta the Reb colonel 'n I was just listenin' in while the ladies were back in the tent. They never told us why they was kickin' us out. Just ta get 'n not come back." By this time the circle had grown so wide

183

that a body could have swung a wagon tongue and never hit a soul. It was all Tim could do to keep a straight face. He had learned early on that once you had the opposition on the run, keep up the assault and he did just that. "If y'all don't mind we could maybe stay with y'all for a few days 'til Miss Savannah gets her strength back. It's been plumb awful the way she been throwin' up every little while. Smells real bad too. Maybe the doc there would spare her a look?" Putting on his best look of concern, Tim approached Savannah and drew her close. "She got the chills but she's burnin' up. Here, feel for yourself." Guiding Savannah toward the lieutenant Tim was relieved to feel her begin to shake uncontrollably and occasionally retch as she bent over.

"I have no interest in feeling her fever or anything else," the officer said as he moved quickly away. "The four of you get on that wagon and make tracks. If you even so much as look in this direction, I will have my men shoot you, now get."

"Yes sir, we're goin' quick as we can, but why won't y'all at least take a look at miss Savannah first?" The game had become amusing to Tim, and the looks of panic on the faces of the Yankee soldiers made it hard to not continue the prodding.

Pulling the revolver from the holster, the officer aimed it at Tim. "If you are still in my sight in the next two minutes, I will personally shoot all four of you. Do I make myself perfectly clear?" Hurrying to help the women to the wagon, Tim simply nodded his head. He didn't want to antagonize the soldier any further, and wondered if he had already carried it a bit too far. Once the women were loaded, Tim almost jumped into the seat and slapped the team into a fast trot. He could not control the smile as he heard Savannah loudly retching in the back.

As soon as they were out of sight of the army camp Connie joined Tim on the seat. "That was some kind of performance back there. Perhaps sometime you could tell me what precipitated such an act, but whatever the reason you saved our bacon."

"I had a feelin' somethin' just didn't seem right from the start back there. Then when that soldier called the lieutenant by his first name, I knew we best get our hides out 'a there. T'ain't no army I know of that allows enlisted men ta call officers by their given name. My Idea is that they're a bunch 'a rag-tag deserters 'n hoodlums that prey on travelers on this deserted road." Tim settled back and pulled the horses to a slower pace. "One thing they did tell me though. Somehow I missed the main road 'n we ain't exactly where we should be. We're still headin' north 'n east 'n that's the direction we want ta be goin'. Problem is that I don't know which way ta turn ta cross the main road. Could be right 'n could be left. I reckon I'll just stay on this one 'n hope for a crossroad."

"You handled the situation extremely well and once again we owe you a great debt of thanks." Connie uncorked one of the canteens and offered Tim a drink. "Tell me if I am right in my assumption. I suspect that we must be in northern territory now. Even ragtags wouldn't dare to be in enemy land with only that small group for protection."

Wiping the dribble of water from his chin Tim handed the canteen back to Connie. "That's 'bout the way I figure things. Sure wish I knew exactly where we is now, but we got ta be somewhere's close ta northern Kentucky by now. I been dead reckonin' by the sun 'n it don't rise 'n set in true east 'n west. We're close ta the right direction, but not exact. We could miss a town by just a mile or two 'n never know it. No town means no railroad ta get you ladies back home."

"You talk like you are not planning to join us in Martindale. All along we assumed that now you have no other relatives, you would come and live with us. There is more than ample room, and I'm sure that you would find living there very enjoyable." The disappointment in Connie's voice was unmistakable. "There will be places to buy new clothes, and restaurants that serve the finest of gourmet foods. Theaters and dances to meet our young ladies, and you will be but a stone throw from the very seat of where our nation was founded. You have my promise that you will not be a bit disappointed if you join us. We owe you so much that there is no way we could ever repay that debt."

"Shucks ma'am," Tim stammered. "There ain't no place for a fella like me 'ceptin' in the wide open. Y'all talk so fancy 'n dress right fine. Why, I'd be nothin' but an embarrassment to y'all. Somehow I just can't see me in no fancy duds 'n spoutin' fancy words. About the first time I ate with my fingers at one 'a your fancy restaurants, y'all would be makin excuses for me 'n I'd be lookin' for a rock ta climb under. Even Hannibal was gettin' too big for me. The best days I ever had was when me 'n Chet was wanderin' through the countryside. I thank ya very much for the offer, but I reckon that once y'all are on the train I'll meander off somewhere's that won't box me in none. I reckon I got a touch of Pa's wander-lust, 'n now ain't nothin' holdin' me in one spot. I'm afraid I wouldn't fit in your world no more than you three ladies'd fit in mine. 'bout like mixin' bacon grease 'n cold water, I reckon. No matter how hard ya stir, the two never do come together."

"I see your point Tim, but we'd still like you to join us. This is really a disappointment. It never occurred to us that you wouldn't be coming home with us. If you should ever change your mind there is always a bed and a place at our table for you. It has been over three years since I have been home and I miss it greatly. I guess where a person is used to living will always be home to them." Connie wasn't certain if the catch in her throat was because of the dust, homesickness, or the unexpected news that had just been presented to her.

"The Mex's have a sayin' like that. 'Mi casa es su casa.'" Tim said, proud to show off his knowledge. "My house is your house. I don't have much of a house out here, but what I have is yours too."

Holding his hand before his eyes he studied the landscape. "I been pushin' the horses pretty good just to get away from that bunch back there. I think when we get to the top 'a that ridge ahead we'll take a breather. Maybe we can get some bearings from up there." Connie climbed back over the seat and joined Ida and Savannah in the back of the wagon.

Alone again, Tim dropped his head against a very fine mist that had only begun to fall. Thankful for anything that would settle the dust, he began to play mind games with himself. He pictured him-self in a tailored suit and starched white shirt, black tie and low cut leather shoes. Riding in a fine carriage he nodded at the pretty young girls who waved at him from the boardwalk. Perhaps that sort of life wouldn't be so bad after all. Second thoughts began to crowd his mind as the trail finally reached the crest of the hill.

Pulling the horses to a halt he turned to the women. "Best take a stretch 'n grab a drink 'a water while I tend the horses. Don't know ....." His voice trailed off as he turned to follow the gaze of the women as they stared behind him. "Well I'll be jigged," he exclaimed, for there nestled in the heart of the basin was a honest to goodness real town. The best part were the glistening twin ribbons of rails that disappeared into the distant hills. It all lay not more than six miles or so below them. Temptation to race toward the first sign of civilization they had seen, since heaven knows when, was soon put behind him. It didn't appear to be much of a town, possibly the size of Hannibal, but it was a town any way. "Well ladies, I reckon if you're gonna pretty up for the gents down there, ya best do it now. It'll take 'bout half hour ta rest 'n tend the horses, 'n I reckon we'll be down there by just 'fore dusk. Yes sir ladies, I think that y'all are on your way home."

It was evident from the look that passed between the women, that Connie had already informed the others of Tim's plans to not accompany them to Martindale. "Are you certain that you won't change your mind Tim? Savannah asked quietly. "I too will have to adjust to the different way of life that awaits me. At least you have been to towns and associated with the people there. That's more than I have ever been allowed to do. Perhaps we could lean on each other for support."

"As pleasurable as that sounds, Miss Savannah, I don't reckon it would work. I been picturin' me in a fancy suit 'n ridin' in a fancy carriage 'n all, but it just ain't me. This beat up old wagon 'n these patched trousers is what I am, not some fancy 'n phony get up. For some folks that's what's expected of 'em, 'cause they're class. Me, I'm nothin but a skinny farm boy 'n that's all I'll ever amount to. You ladies have treated me like an equal, 'n for that I'm mighty grateful, but it only worked 'cause of where we are. It wouldn't be the same on your stompin' grounds."

"Stomping grounds," Connie repeated, "I have never heard that expression used when referring to ones home. Honestly Tim, I don't know what we would ever do without you. We treat you as an equal because you are exactly that. You have taught us to survive where we would have certainly perished."

"I don't reckon that y'all have ever seen prairie chickens 'round courtin' time. Them ol' roosters puff up 'n dance around the hens a tryin' ta attract one. Far as a eye can see is nothin' but struttin' 'n dancin' birds. Where they do that's their stompin' grounds. Some

Indian dances are done after the steps the prairie chickens take. See, I know all that useless stuff, but when it comes ta bein' in your fancy world, I'd be a failure. I love all y'all like family, but I reckon it'll be best for us ta part down there. I promise that I won't never forget y'all 'n the way ya tried ta look after me." Turning to look over the valley below, a faint rainbow arched over the town and disappeared behind the far hills.

Epilogue.

"Well folks, that's 'bout the end 'a the story, least ways the way I remember it 'n the way it was told ta me. T'ain't much else ta say. When we got ta that town it turned out ta be Paducah, Kentuck. The next train north was leavin' in just two days. Some Yankee officer kept eyeballin' Miss Connie, 'n he arraigned for the ladies ta get a ticket ta Philadelphia on the next train out. They begged for me ta go back with 'em 'n live in their house. Shucks, I ain't got no business livin' in some big house 'n havin' three women tellin me what ta do, not by a long shot. If I'm gonna be the man 'a the family, I got ta start actin' like one, even if I am the whole family now. After all I am sixteen, well fifteen, but my birthday's in five months 'n twelve days so that makes me closer ta sixteen than fifteen. When the ladies left they was nice enough ta give me this here wagon 'n team, 'long with 'nuff gold spendin' money ta keep me goin' for quite a spell. I got mine hid good 'n proper too. Wonder where they got all them gold coins? Sure didn't know that's what I pulled out 'a that coffin. We been trapsin' all over the country with it 'tween my feet all the time.

Seems the war was on the tail end 'a windin' down 'n it looks like the South took a whippin'. They's still lots 'a hotspots, 'n the Yankees are in places we never thought they'd ever get to. They's been a lot 'a good men from both sides die in this here war, 'n even innocent folks hurt 'cause of it. Some gets burned out, while others get plain killed, or worse. Some folks sayin' when this one's over they ain't gonna be no more wars. Sure hope they's right 'bout

189

that. This thing makes it hard on everybody. Just don't look like there's no winners ta me.

I got the team all hitched so I reckon I'll head out. Might mosey around Hannibal for a spell, 'n then head out west. Seems ta me that I got just as good a chance as anybody ta pick up all that silver that's layin' around. Who knows? Maybe someday I can have me a big house 'n plantation, just like that Master Ham had. 'Master Tim.' Now don't that just have a grand sound ta it?

One other thing 'fore I quit bendin' your ear 'n head out. About that fella what shot Chet. I think figured how that timber rattler got in his bed. I'll just bet that there weren't no live snake nohow. I bet some no account killed that rattler, sneaked inta the tent while that fella was out exercizin' 'n coiled it up under the blanket just like the real thing. If y'all got in bed with one, would ya stop 'n check if the critter was breathin' 'n say 'Hello' ta it? I sure wouldn't. I bet he figured that fella'd do just what he done 'n run. I reckon the one what put it there just went about his business in camp. Don't that sound 'bout right ta y'all?

Ma always told me that I'd talk the leg off a dead horse 'n I reckon I bent your ear long 'nuff. Right nice talkin' ta y'all 'n sure happy ta meet up with ya. Bye for now 'n maybe we'll run inta each other again someday. 'til then God Bless.'"

by Timothy B. Baxter.